Eco-Wings Birds And Their Roles In Sustaining Biodiversity

By
Ehsan Sheroy

INDEX Page Nos

INTRODUCTION

Biodiversity, the assortment of life on The planet, is essential to the wellbeing and versatility of environments. Inside this complicated snare of life, birds assume an essential part in supporting biodiversity. From their different transformations to different natural surroundings to the fundamental environment administrations they give, birds contribute altogether to the equilibrium and prosperity of our planet. This investigation of "Eco-Wings" digs into the mind boggling connections among birds and biodiversity, inspecting their jobs, the difficulties they face, and the preservation endeavors fundamental for their endurance.

Avian Variety:

The universe of birds is amazingly assorted, with more than 10,000 species occupying different environments, from tropical rainforests to cold tundras. Every species is interestingly adjusted to its current circumstance, exhibiting a striking cluster of varieties, sizes, and ways of behaving. Investigating avian variety permits us to see the value in the unpredictable embroidery of life and comprehend the particular jobs various birds play inside environments.

Environment Administrations Given by Birds:

Birds give important biological system benefits that add to the general wellbeing and usefulness of environments. One of the essential administrations is fertilization, as many plants rely upon birds to move dust between blossoms, working with proliferation. Birds likewise assume an imperative part in seed dispersal, helping with the recovery of woodlands and keeping up with plant variety. Also, they go about as normal vermin regulators, assisting with holding bug populaces under tight restraints and keeping up with environmental equilibrium. Birds further add to supplement burnning and soil wellbeing through exercises like rummaging and settling.

Birds as Signs of Natural Wellbeing:

Birds are delicate to ecological changes, making them strong marks of environment wellbeing. Observing bird populaces permits researchers to evaluate the effect of human exercises, environmental change, and living space debasement. Changes in bird conduct, populace size, or relocation examples can flag more extensive changes in natural circumstances, filling in as early admonitions for likely biological issues.

Dangers to Avian Biodiversity:

Notwithstanding their versatility, birds face various dangers that imperil their endurance and, therefore, biodiversity.

Natural surroundings misfortune because of human exercises, for example, deforestation and urbanization is a critical concern, dividing bird environments and restricting their admittance to assets. Environmental change represents another significant danger, influencing transient examples, rearing seasons, and the accessibility of food sources. Contamination, from pesticides to plastic waste, likewise negatively affects bird populaces, influencing their wellbeing and conceptive achievement. Obtrusive species further fuel these difficulties by contending with local birds for assets.

Protection Endeavors:
Perceiving the significance of birds in supporting biodiversity, protection endeavors are in progress around the world. Laying out safeguarded regions and untamed life holds helps protect basic living spaces for birds. Environment reclamation drives center around fixing biological systems harmed by human exercises, furnishing birds with an opportunity to recuperate. Worldwide cooperation is fundamental, as transitory birds navigate borders, stressing the requirement for composed preservation procedures. Connecting with neighborhood networks through resident science and instructive projects upgrades preservation mindfulness and guarantees feasible practices.

Examples of overcoming adversity in Bird Preservation:
Notwithstanding the difficulties, there have been prominent accomplishments in bird protection. Species recuperation programs, like those for the California Condor or the Bald Eagle, exhibit the potential for switching declines when purposeful endeavors are made. Renewed introduction programs, where hostage reproduced birds are delivered into the wild, have effectively restored populaces of fundamentally jeopardized species. The examples gained from these examples of overcoming adversity give important experiences into successful protection procedures.

The Job of Birds in Ecotourism:
Birdwatching, a well known type of ecotourism, brings monetary advantages as well as adds to bird protection. Mindful the travel industry rehearses guarantee negligible effect on bird natural surroundings, and the income created from birdwatching visits can finance nearby protection drives. Local area commitment in ecotourism advances the significance of saving normal regions and gives motivators to nearby networks to partake in protection endeavors effectively.

Future Difficulties and Amazing open doors:
As we plan ahead, arising difficulties undermine bird populaces and, likewise, biodiversity. Understanding these difficulties is pivotal for creating proactive preservation measures.

Advancements in protection science, like the utilization of satellite innovation and man-made brainpower, offer new apparatuses for observing bird populaces and tending to natural dangers. Notwithstanding, tending to the underlying drivers of territory misfortune, environmental change, and contamination stays central for reasonable bird protection.

A.   Definition of Biodiversity

Biodiversity, short for natural variety, is a term that typifies the assortment of life on Earth at all levels, from qualities to environments. It is a proportion of the lavishness and intricacy of living creatures and their cooperations. This complete investigation means to unwind the complexities of biodiversity, looking at its definition, importance, and the elements affecting its examples and elements.

Meaning of Biodiversity:

Biodiversity envelops the assortment of life on The planet, including the variety of species, hereditary variety inside species, and the variety of environments. At its center, biodiversity mirrors the overflow and appropriation of living creatures across various conditions. This complex idea is in many cases separated into three principal parts:

Species Variety:

Species variety alludes to the wide range of species in a specific environment or on the whole planet. It incorporates the quantity of species present, their relative overflow, and the range of biological jobs they play. High species variety is characteristic of a solid and strong environment, as various species add to different natural capabilities.

Hereditary Variety:

Hereditary variety exists inside species and alludes to the range of qualities and hereditary attributes inside a populace. It is essential for the versatility and endurance of an animal categories notwithstanding natural changes. Hereditary variety permits populaces to develop and adjust to new circumstances, upgrading their capacity to oppose infections, bothers, and other natural difficulties.

Biological system Variety:

Biological system variety relates to the range of environments present on The planet. Biological systems are complicated, cooperating frameworks that incorporate living creatures and their actual surroundings. Various biological systems, like backwoods, prairies, wetlands, and coral reefs, add to the general biodiversity of the planet. Every environment has remarkable species arrangements and biological cycles.

Meaning of Biodiversity:
Biodiversity is of central significance for the prosperity of the planet and its occupants. A few key viewpoints feature its importance:

Biological Security:
Biodiversity adds to the dependability and versatility of biological systems. Various biological systems are better prepared to endure unsettling influences, like outrageous climate occasions, illnesses, or obtrusive species. The overt repetitiveness of species inside environments guarantees that assuming one animal categories declines or vanishes, others can step in to satisfy comparable biological jobs, keeping up with the general equilibrium.

Environment Administrations:
Biodiversity gives fundamental environment benefits that help human prosperity. These administrations incorporate clean air and water, fertilization of yields, guideline of environment, and deterioration of natural matter. Solid and different environments are more useful and versatile, improving their capacity to offer these pivotal types of assistance.

Social and Tasteful Worth:
Biodiversity holds social importance for some networks all over the planet. Native societies frequently have profound associations with explicit species or biological systems, integrating them into ceremonies, customs, and day to day existence. Also, the stylish worth of biodiversity adds to the pleasure and motivation got from nature, affecting craftsmanship, writing, and diversion.

Therapeutic Assets:
Numerous species add to the improvement of drugs and clinical medicines. Biodiversity fills in as a huge supply of hereditary assets that can be saddled for the revelation of new medications and treatments. The deficiency of biodiversity might restrict future open doors for clinical headways.

Factors Impacting Biodiversity:
Biodiversity isn't appropriated equally across the planet, and different elements impact its examples and elements. Understanding these elements is essential for powerful preservation and the board. A portion of the key impacts include:

Environment:
Environment assumes a critical part in deciding the sorts of species that can flourish in various districts.

Temperature, precipitation, and other climatic elements shape the dissemination of environments and the species they support. Environmental change represents a developing danger to biodiversity by modifying natural surroundings and disturbing biological connections.

Natural surroundings Misfortune and Discontinuity:
Human exercises, like deforestation, urbanization, and horticultural extension, lead to natural surroundings misfortune and fracture. This disturbs environments, uproots species, and diminishes the accessibility of appropriate living spaces. Living space misfortune is an essential driver of animal types elimination and a significant danger to biodiversity.

Contamination:
Contamination, whether from modern exercises, agribusiness, or metropolitan spillover, negatively affects biodiversity. Pollutants can aggregate in biological systems, influencing the strength of living beings and disturbing environmental cycles. Synthetic poisons, plastics, and supplement overflow add to the corruption of environments and the decay of species.

Overexploitation:
The overharvesting of species for food, medication, pets, or different purposes can prompt populace declines and even eradication. Overfishing, unlawful natural life exchange, and unreasonable logging are instances of exercises that can exhaust populaces and upset biological systems.

Intrusive Species:
The acquaintance of non-local species with new conditions can have extreme ramifications for local biodiversity. Intrusive species may outcompete local species for assets, present illnesses, or disturb biological cycles. Their presence can prompt the decay or termination of local species.

Protection of Biodiversity:
Perceiving the significance of biodiversity and the dangers it faces, preservation endeavors are in progress around the world. These endeavors intend to safeguard and economically oversee environments, save imperiled species, and advance capable asset use. Key protection procedures include:

Safeguarded Regions:
Laying out safeguarded regions, for example, public parks and untamed life saves, helps defend basic living spaces and give asylum to assorted species. Safeguarded regions additionally act as living labs for logical exploration and ecological training.

Natural surroundings Rebuilding:
Endeavors to reestablish corrupted territories center around restoring normal biological systems and working on their versatility. Rebuilding projects include establishing local vegetation, eliminating obtrusive species, and executing supportable land the board rehearses.

Regulation and Approaches:
Legislatures and global associations assume a significant part in biodiversity preservation through the execution of regulations and strategies. These guidelines plan to control territory obliteration, direct hunting and fishing, and address different exercises that compromise biodiversity.

Local area Commitment:
Including nearby networks in protection endeavors is fundamental for long haul achievement. Native information and customary practices frequently contribute important bits of knowledge to preservation systems. Connecting with networks in supportable asset the executives advances the conjunction of human exercises and biodiversity.

Exploration and Observing:
Continuous examination is fundamental for figuring out the elements of biodiversity and surveying the viability of protection measures. Observing projects track changes in species populaces, living space conditions, and different pointers, giving important information to versatile administration.

B.   Importance of Biodiversity for Ecosystem Health

Biodiversity, the assortment of life on The planet, is unpredictably connected to the wellbeing and working of biological systems. The complicated snare of associations among species, the hereditary variety inside populaces, and the range of environments by and large add to the dependability, strength, and efficiency of normal frameworks. This investigation digs into the significant significance of biodiversity for environment wellbeing, looking at the horde manners by which assorted living things support the equilibrium and usefulness of the planet's biological systems.

Natural Steadiness and Flexibility:
Biodiversity is a vital determinant of environmental dependability and flexibility.
Biological systems with high biodiversity will generally be more steady, meaning they
can endure and recuperate from unsettling influences all the more really. The presence
of assorted species with various natural jobs gives a type of protection against
ecological changes. In such frameworks, on the off chance that one animal varieties is
harmed by an aggravation, others might have the option to make up for the misfortune,
keeping up with generally speaking biological system dependability.
For instance, in a woods biological system, different tree species might have changing
resiliences to bugs, sicknesses, or outrageous climate occasions. On the off chance
that one animal categories is defenseless to a specific danger, others might stay
unaffected, forestalling the breakdown of the whole environment. This overt
repetitiveness in natural capabilities is a sign of biodiverse frameworks, guaranteeing
that biological systems can adjust to evolving conditions.

Efficiency and Supplement Cycling:
Biodiversity assumes a vital part in biological system efficiency and supplement cycling.
Inside environments, various species add to the spinning of supplements through
different organic cycles. For example, plants assimilate supplements from the dirt, and
when these plants are eaten by herbivores, the supplements are moved through the
pecking order. Decomposers then, at that point, separate natural matter, returning
supplements to the dirt for plant take-up.
The variety of species engaged with these cycles upgrades the effectiveness of
supplement cycling. Every species might have extraordinary transformations that impact
supplement accessibility and take-up. In biodiverse biological systems, the mind
boggling connections between species add to a more effective reusing of supplements,
cultivating higher efficiency.

Variation to Ecological Changes:
Biodiversity is a wellspring of hereditary variety, which is significant for the
transformation of species to changing ecological circumstances. Inside populaces of a
solitary animal types, hereditary variety considers varieties in characteristics like
protection from illnesses, resistance to temperature limits, or the capacity to flourish in
various soil types.
Despite environmental change, for instance, species with more noteworthy hereditary
variety are bound to have people with attributes that can endure modified temperature
or precipitation designs. This flexibility is crucial for the drawn out endurance of species
and their capacity to continue despite natural difficulties.

Fertilization and Generation:

Many plants depend on creatures, especially bugs and birds, for fertilization.
Biodiversity is basic for guaranteeing the accessibility of pollinators, which assume a
crucial part in the proliferation of blossoming plants. A different local area of pollinators,
including honey bees, butterflies, birds, and bats, guarantees that an extensive variety
of plant species can repeat.
The mind boggling connections among plants and their pollinators have co-advanced
over the long haul, prompting specific transformations and conditions. Loss of
biodiversity, particularly the downfall of pollinator species, can upset these connections,
prompting a decrease in plant conceptive achievement. This, thusly, influences the
accessibility of food and territory for different species in the biological system.

Infection Guideline:

Biodiversity can likewise assume a part in managing the spread of illnesses. In
biological systems with high biodiversity, there is much of the time a weakening impact,
where the presence of different species can lessen the predominance of sicknesses.
This is especially pertinent in frameworks where a few animal groups go about as
repositories for sicknesses that influence others.
For instance, in a woods biological system, a different local area of tree species might
restrict the spread of a specific parasitic microorganism. Assuming a microbe basically
influences one tree animal varieties, the presence of other tree species that are not
powerless can forestall the fast spread of the illness. This dynamic is a fundamental part
of biological system wellbeing, forestalling the uncontrolled multiplication of sicknesses
that could demolish whole environments.

Environment Guideline and Carbon Sequestration:

Biodiverse environments add to environment guideline and carbon sequestration.
Timberlands, for example, are essential for relieving environmental change as they
ingest and store a lot of carbon dioxide through photosynthesis. The variety of tree
species in a backwoods improves its capacity to sequester carbon, as various species
have different development rates and carbon stockpiling limits.
Furthermore, wetlands and seas, which harbor different networks of life, additionally
assume huge parts in controlling environment by retaining and putting away carbon.
The deficiency of biodiversity in these biological systems can think twice about ability to
sequester carbon, adding to the amassing of ozone depleting substances in the
environment and fueling environmental change.

C.   Focus on Birds as Key Contributors to Biodiversity

Birds, with their lively plumage, musical melodies, and different variations, stand as key supporters of the perplexing embroidery of biodiversity. From backwoods to deserts, mountains to seas, birds possess practically every environment on The planet, assuming fundamental parts in biological system elements. This investigation digs into the meaning of birds as key supporters of biodiversity, inspecting their different natural capabilities, the novel transformations that characterize avian variety, and the interconnected connections that tight spot them to the wellbeing of biological systems.

Biological Elements of Birds:

Birds satisfy a bunch of biological capabilities that are vital for the wellbeing and equilibrium of environments. A portion of their key jobs include:

Fertilization: Many bird species, including hummingbirds and sunbirds, are proficient pollinators. As they feed on nectar, their heads come into contact with blossoms, working with the exchange of dust between plants. This cycle is fundamental for the multiplication of various blossoming plant species, adding to the upkeep of plant biodiversity.

Seed Dispersal: Birds assume a huge part in seed dispersal by consuming leafy foods saving seeds in new areas through their droppings. This cycle supports the colonization of new regions by plant species, adding to the recovery of timberlands and the foundation of different plant networks.

Bug Control: Insectivorous birds, for example, songbirds and flycatchers, assist with controlling bug populaces, adding to the guideline of nuisance species. By benefiting from bugs, birds assume a crucial part in keeping up with the equilibrium of hunter prey connections inside environments.

Supplement Cycling: Birds add to supplement burnning through exercises like rummaging and settling. For instance, seabird settlements are known for focusing supplements on islands through their guano, improving the dirt and supporting the development of vegetation.

Avian Variations and Variety:

The amazing variety of birds is obvious in their transformations to different conditions and environmental specialties. These transformations have permitted birds to colonize different living spaces and take advantage of a large number of assets. A few striking models include:

Bill Morphology: Birds show an enormous variety in snout shapes and sizes, mirroring their particular taking care of propensities. For example, the long, thin bills of hummingbirds are adjusted for tasting nectar from blossoms, while the strong, snared bills of raptors are intended for tearing tissue.

Relocation: Many bird species attempt momentous significant distance movements, voyaging large number of kilometers among reproducing and wintering grounds. This variation permits them to take advantage of occasional assets and stay away from cruel natural circumstances.

Vocalizations: Birds utilize various vocalizations for correspondence, mating, and laying out domains. The intricacy of bird melodies shifts across species, with some, similar to the lyrebird, displaying a surprising cluster of emulating capacities.

Plumage and Cover: Plumage fills different needs, from drawing in mates to giving disguise. Birds like the peacock grandstand luxurious plumage for romance presentations, while others, similar to the potoo, depend on cover to mix flawlessly with their environmental elements.
The variety of avian transformations is a demonstration of the developmental outcome of birds and their capacity to take advantage of biological specialties in various environments.

Marker Species for Biological system Wellbeing:
Birds act as significant marks of biological system wellbeing because of their aversion to ecological changes. Changes in bird populaces, conduct, or conveyance can flag more extensive changes in biological circumstances. Checking bird species can give bits of knowledge into the effects of human exercises, environmental change, and territory corruption.

Movement Examples: Adjustments in bird relocation designs, like changes in timing or courses, may demonstrate shifts in environment or territory accessibility. Concentrating on these examples assists researchers with surveying the impacts of environmental change on bird populaces.

Rearing Achievement: The conceptive progress of bird species is many times affected by the accessibility of reasonable natural surroundings and food sources. Decreases in reproducing achievement can be demonstrative of environment corruption or the effect of poisons.

Presence of Jeopardized Species: The presence or nonappearance of specific bird species can act as a mark of generally environment wellbeing. Jeopardized or compromised bird species might feature regions requiring quick protection consideration.
By going about as sentinels for natural changes, birds contribute important data that guides in the definition of protection procedures and the conservation of generally speaking biodiversity.

Financial and Social Significance:
Birds hold financial and social importance for human social orders all over the planet. Their significance stretches out past environmental jobs to regions, for example,

Eco-The travel industry: Birdwatching is a well known sporting movement and a critical part of eco-the travel industry. Numerous districts draw in sightseers anxious to notice assorted bird species in their normal natural surroundings, adding to nearby economies.

Horticulture: Birds add to farming by giving nuisance control administrations. Insectivorous birds assist with holding bug populaces under control, diminishing the requirement for substance pesticides.

Social Imagery: Birds hold social imagery in different social orders, frequently addressing opportunity, magnificence, or otherworldliness. They highlight conspicuously in craftsmanship, writing, and folklore, mirroring the profound associations among people and birds.
Perceiving the financial and social worth of birds highlights the significance of saving their territories and keeping up with biodiversity to support the two environments and human social orders.

Chapter 1
Avian Diversity

Avian variety, the huge swath of bird species populating the Earth, is a demonstration of the developmental resourcefulness of these noteworthy animals. From the littlest hummingbird to the glorious gooney bird, birds occupy different environments across the globe, showing a shocking cluster of varieties, shapes, ways of behaving, and variations. This investigation digs into the multi-layered universe of avian variety, looking at the elements impacting it, the natural jobs played by various bird species, and the preservation challenges looked by this padded domain.

I. Outline of Avian Variety
A. Meaning of Avian Variety:
Avian variety envelops the assortment of bird species possessing various areas, biological systems, and specialties around the world. With north of 10,000 perceived species, birds display a shocking scope of sizes, shapes, varieties, and ways of behaving. This variety is molded by developmental cycles, including regular choice, variation to explicit conditions, and the mind boggling transaction of natural connections.

B. Scientific categorization and Order:
Birds are ordered into different scientific classifications in view of their developmental connections. The progressive arrangement of characterization incorporates classes, orders, families, genera, and species. Understanding avian scientific classification gives experiences into the developmental history and connections among various bird species.

C. Conveyance of Bird Species:
Birds are conveyed across all landmasses, from polar districts to tropical rainforests, and from high mountain reaches to tremendous sea fields. The conveyance of bird species is affected by variables like environment, natural surroundings accessibility, and the presence of explicit food sources. Endemism, where certain species are limited to specific geographic regions, adds intricacy to avian circulation designs.

II. Variations and Specializations in Avian Variety
A. Mouth and Bill Variety:
The variety of nose and bill shapes among birds mirrors their transformation to explicit taking care of systems.

From the long, testing bills of shorebirds to the hearty, seed-breaking bills of finches, every transformation improves a bird's capacity to take advantage of its favored food source.

B. Taking care of Procedures:
Avian variety is further obvious in the different taking care of systems utilized by various species. Flesh eating birds, like raptors, have sharp claws and snouts for catching and consuming prey. Herbivores, like parrots, have particular bills for popping nuts and seeds. Nectar feeders, similar to hummingbirds, have long, specific bills for extricating nectar from blossoms.

C. Transitory Way of behaving:
Movement is a boundless peculiarity among birds, permitting them to take advantage of occasional assets and keep away from negative circumstances. A few birds, similar to the Cold Tern, embrace remarkable significant distance movements, covering large number of kilometers among rearing and wintering grounds.

D. Romance Presentations and Plumage:
Avian variety reaches out to romance showcases and plumage, which assume essential parts in mate choice and conceptive achievement. Elaborate moves, brilliant plumage, and unpredictable vocalizations are all essential for the assorted collection of romance ways of behaving showed by various bird species.

III. Bird Families and Species
A. Waterfowl (Anatidae):
The waterfowl family incorporates ducks, geese, and swans. These birds are all around adjusted to amphibian conditions, with webbed feet for swimming and fiddling, and concentrated bills for sifting food from the water.

B. Raptors (Accipitridae and Falconidae):
Raptors, including birds, falcons, hawks, and vultures, are portrayed by strong snouts and claws. They are dominant hunters, assuming fundamental parts in controlling prey populaces and keeping up with environment balance.

C. Passerines (Passeriformes):
Passerines, or roosting birds, make up the biggest request of birds and incorporate sparrows, finches, robins, and warblers. Their different mouth shapes and taking care of propensities add to their progress in different conditions.

D. Hummingbirds (Trochilidae):

Hummingbirds are known for their momentous floating skills and energetic plumage. Their long, specific bills are adjusted for separating nectar from blossoms, making them significant pollinators.

E. Parrots (Psittacidae):

Parrots are portrayed by areas of strength for them, bills, zygodactyl feet (two toes pointing forward and two in reverse), and dynamic plumage. They are tracked down in tropical and subtropical locales and are known for their knowledge and capacity to copy sounds.

F. Penguins (Spheniscidae):

Penguins are flightless birds adjusted to marine life. Their wings have developed into flippers for proficient swimming, and their plumage gives protection against cold temperatures.

IV. Natural Jobs of Birds
A. Fertilization Administrations:

Many bird species, including hummingbirds, sunbirds, and honeyeaters, add to fertilization by moving dust between blossoms. This mutualistic relationship is significant for the generation of various plant species, supporting by and large biological system wellbeing.

B. Seed Dispersal:

Birds assume a crucial part in seed dispersal by consuming foods grown from the ground seeds in new areas through their droppings. This interaction is fundamental for the recovery of woods and the foundation of plant networks.

C. Bug Control:

Insectivorous birds, like songbirds, flycatchers, and swallows, assist with controlling bug populaces, adding to the guideline of irritation species and advancing by and large biological system balance.

D. Supplement Cycling:

Seabird states, including those of gooney birds and penguins, focus supplements on islands through their guano. This supplement input improves soil fruitfulness, supporting the development of vegetation and adding to supplement cycling in marine environments.

V. Dangers to Avian Variety
A. Environment Misfortune and Discontinuity:
Human exercises, like deforestation, urbanization, and farming, lead to environment misfortune and discontinuity, influencing bird populaces by restricting their admittance to appropriate living spaces and assets.

B. Environmental Change:
Environmental change represents a huge danger to avian variety by modifying temperature and precipitation designs, influencing movement courses, reproducing seasons, and the accessibility of food sources.

C. Contamination:
Different types of contamination, including compound poisons, plastic waste, and oil slicks, influence bird populaces by debasing their living spaces and food sources, prompting unfriendly wellbeing impacts.

D. Obtrusive Species:
The presentation of non-local species can upset biological systems and adversely influence local bird populaces by vieing for assets, presenting sicknesses, or originating before on local species.

VI. Preservation of Avian Variety
A. Safeguarded Regions and Stores:
Laying out and keeping up with safeguarded regions, public parks, and untamed life saves is essential for protecting territories and giving places of refuge to different bird species.

B. Environment Rebuilding:
Environment rebuilding drives center around fixing biological systems harmed by human exercises, like reforestation, wetland reclamation, and the evacuation of intrusive species.

C. Global Cooperation:
Global participation is fundamental for the protection of transitory bird species that cross numerous nations. Cooperative endeavors and arrangements work with the assurance of basic territories along relocation courses.

D. Schooling and Mindfulness:
Instructing the general population about the significance of avian variety and its preservation cultivates a feeling of obligation and energizes reasonable practices.

Protection mindfulness drives can incorporate instructive projects, birdwatching occasions, and resident science projects.

E. Exploration and Checking:
Continuous exploration is significant for checking bird populaces, figuring out their natural jobs, and surveying the viability of preservation endeavors. Propels in innovation, for example, bird GPS beacons and remote detecting, upgrade the limit with respect to research and checking.

1.1   Overview of Bird Species

Birds, with their captivating variety in structure, capability, and conduct, comprise an energetic and vital part of the world's biological systems. From the taking off hawks to the coordinated hummingbirds, the worldwide avian domain envelops north of 10,000 perceived species, each interestingly adjusted to its current circumstance. This exhaustive investigation expects to give an outline of bird species, diving into their grouping, biological jobs, transformations, and the protection challenges they face.

I. Characterization of Bird Species
A. Scientific classification and Systematics:
Birds, individuals from the class Aves, are characterized in light of a progressive arrangement of scientific categorization. This framework incorporates different levels, like requests, families, genera, and species. Understanding the arrangement of bird species gives experiences into their developmental connections and shared qualities.

B. Orders of Birds:
Birds are sorted into various orders, each addressing a gathering of animal types with normal qualities. A few unmistakable orders include:

Passeriformes (Roosting Birds): The biggest request, described by the presence of a specific rear toe for roosting.

Accipitriformes (Flying predators): Raptors like birds, falcons, and vultures, known for their strong bills and claws.

Columbiformes (Pigeons and Birds): Incorporates species with exceptional transformations for seed-eating and romance presentations.

C. Family Variety:

Families inside orders further group birds in view of shared attributes. For example, inside the request Passeriformes, families like Tyrannidae (dictator flycatchers) and Fringillidae (finches) address unmistakable gatherings with exceptional elements.

D. Class and Species:

The family and species levels of grouping give explicit IDs to individual birds. For instance, the American Robin is named Turdus migratorius, where Turdus is the class and migratorius is the species.

II. Worldwide Dispersion of Bird Species
A. Biogeographic Locales:

Bird species show different dissemination designs across the globe, affected by variables like environment, living space accessibility, and developmental history. Biogeographic districts, as Nearctic, Palearctic, Neotropical, and Australasian, characterize regions with unmistakable avian arrays.

B. Endemism:

Many bird species are endemic to explicit locales, meaning they are found no place else on the planet. Endemism adds a layer of intricacy to avian dissemination, featuring the significance of saving extraordinary natural surroundings to protect particular species.

C. Relocation Courses:

Relocation is a typical peculiarity among birds, with species voyaging immense distances among rearing and wintering grounds. Striking relocation courses, for example, the East Asian-Australasian Flyway, feature the unimaginable excursions embraced by transient bird species.

III. Environmental Jobs and Transformations
A. Taking care of Procedures:

Birds display assorted taking care of procedures, reflecting variations to their environmental specialties. Models include:

Carnivores: Raptors like hawks and hawks with specific mouths and claws for catching prey.

Herbivores: Finches with hearty mouths adjusted for breaking seeds and removing plant materials.

Insectivores: Larks and flycatchers with slim bills for getting bugs in flight.

B. Conceptive Techniques:
Avian conceptive techniques fluctuate, enveloping different settling ways of behaving, romance shows, and mating frameworks. Pilgrim nesters, like seabirds, gather in huge numbers to raise, while lone nesters, similar to raptors, lay out individual regions.

C. Vocalizations:
Vocalizations serve fundamental jobs in correspondence, mate fascination, and domain foundation. Larks, similar to thrushes and songbirds, are known for intricate melodies, while parrots are praised for their capacity to imitate a large number of sounds.

D. Movement and Route:
Movement is a momentous variation that permits birds to take advantage of occasional assets and keep away from brutal circumstances. Navigational capacities, frequently directed by divine prompts, milestones, and Earth's attractive field, empower transient species to set out on exact excursions.

E. Cover and Plumage:
Plumage assumes a pivotal part in avian variations, giving disguise, warm protection, and correspondence. Species like the ptarmigan change plumage tone with the seasons, while birds of heaven show excessive plumage for romance presentations.

IV. Outstanding Bird Families and Species
A. Warblers (Passeriformes):
Larks, or passerines, address the biggest request of birds, with different families like thrushes (Turdidae), songbirds (Parulidae), and finches (Fringillidae). The mind boggling vocalizations and versatile ways of behaving of larks make them a focal point of ornithological exploration and birdwatching.

B. Flying predators (Accipitriformes and Falconiformes):
Raptors, including hawks (Accipitridae) and birds of prey (Falconidae), are dominant hunters with particular variations for hunting. Their sharp vision, strong claws, and taking off capacities add to their prosperity as top hunters in different biological systems.

C. Waterfowl (Anatidae):
Ducks, geese, and swans are individuals from the waterfowl family, known for their oceanic transformations. Transient examples, fiddling ways of behaving, and complicated romance showcases portray these birds, making them conspicuous elements in wetland environments.

D. Parrots (Psittacidae):
Parrots, with their vivid plumage and surprising knowledge, occupy tropical and subtropical districts. Known for their capacity to impersonate human discourse and show complex critical thinking abilities, parrots are appealling and socially captivating species.

E. Hummingbirds (Trochilidae):
Hummingbirds are little, radiant marvels with one of a kind transformations for floating flight and nectar taking care of. Their particular noses and fast wing beats make them key pollinators in environments going from rainforests to parched deserts.

V. Dangers to Bird Species
A. Living space Misfortune and Debasement:
Human exercises, including deforestation, urbanization, and agribusiness, lead to the annihilation and discontinuity of bird environments, decreasing accessible assets and presenting huge dangers to numerous species.

B. Environmental Change:
Modifications in temperature, precipitation designs, and the recurrence of outrageous climate occasions because of environmental change influence bird species by influencing food accessibility, settling achievement, and relocation timing.

C. Contamination:
Contamination, including pesticides, plastics, and foreign substances in water bodies, presents direct dangers to bird wellbeing and in a roundabout way influences food sources. Species subject to explicit prey or living spaces might be especially helpless.

D. Intrusive Species:
The presentation of non-local species can disturb environments, prompting rivalry for assets, predation on local species, and the spread of infections. Obtrusive species add to decreases in local bird populaces.

VI. Protection Systems
A. Safeguarded Regions and Stores:
Laying out and keeping up with safeguarded regions, public parks, and untamed life saves assume an essential part in protecting natural surroundings and giving places of refuge to different bird species.

B. Living space Reclamation:
Living space reclamation drives center around fixing environments harmed by human exercises, including reforestation, wetland rebuilding, and the expulsion of intrusive species.

C. Exploration and Observing:
Continuous examination is fundamental for checking bird populaces, grasping their natural jobs, and surveying the adequacy of preservation endeavors. Innovative headways, for example, GPS beacons and remote detecting, improve research capacities.

D. Schooling and Promotion:
Public mindfulness and commitment are basic for effective bird protection. Instructive projects, birdwatching occasions, and backing endeavors bring issues to light about the significance of birds and the dangers they face.

E. Worldwide Coordinated effort:
Global collaboration is essential for monitoring transitory species that cross different nations. Cooperative endeavors and arrangements work with the assurance of basic living spaces along relocation courses.

1.2   Distribution and Habitats of Birds

Birds, with their capacity to navigate landmasses, possess assorted conditions, and adjust to fluctuated natural specialties, exhibit an unrivaled conveyance across the globe. The investigation of the dispersion and territories of birds isn't just an investigation of their geographic ranges yet in addition a knowledge into the mind boggling associations between avian species and their surroundings. This complete investigation digs into the elements impacting the dispersion of birds, the different territories they possess, and the biological meaning of these connections.

I. Factors Affecting the Dispersion of Birds
A. Environment and Temperature:
The dissemination of bird species is emphatically impacted by climatic circumstances and temperature slopes. Various species show inclinations for explicit temperature ranges, deciding their presence in polar, calm, tropical, or dry areas. For instance, penguins flourish in cool Antarctic environments, while toucans are adjusted to the glow of tropical rainforests.

B. Elevation and Geology:
Height assumes a pivotal part in bird circulation, with species adjusted to explicit rises. Rocky areas, like the Himalayas, grandstand particular avian networks at various altitudinal zones. Birds adjust to differing oxygen levels, temperature, and vegetation as they rise or plunge in height.

C. Accessibility of Water:
The nearness and accessibility of water are key variables affecting bird appropriation. Waterbirds, like ducks and herons, are frequently connected with wetlands, lakes, and streams. Beach front regions give environments to seabirds, while deserts and parched locales are home to species adjusted to water shortage.

D. Vegetation and Living space Types:
The sort of vegetation and natural surroundings altogether impact bird dissemination. Timberland abiding species, like woodpeckers and owls, are adjusted to lush conditions, while field birds, similar to warblers and sparrows, flourish in open scenes. Birds display specialization in view of the accessibility of explicit vegetation types, from mangroves to coniferous timberlands.

E. Food Accessibility and Assets:
The circulation of birds is firmly connected to the accessibility of food assets. Insectivorous birds might be more plentiful in regions with a high thickness of bugs, while granivores are tracked down in locales with bountiful seeds. Accessibility of reasonable settling locales and reproducing assets likewise assumes a part in deciding conveyance designs.

F. Movement Courses:
Many bird species attempt occasional movements, following explicit courses among rearing and wintering grounds. The accessibility of appropriate visit destinations along relocation courses is basic for the progress of these excursions. Changes in relocation examples can demonstrate shifts in ecological circumstances.

II. Different Living spaces of Birds
A. Earthbound Living spaces:

Woods:
Tropical Rainforests: Home to a surprising variety of bird species, including toucans, parrots, and different warblers. Shade inhabitants, understory birds, and ground-scavenging species add to the multifaceted woven artwork of tropical woodland environments.

Mild and Boreal Woodlands: Host to woodpeckers, owls, and songbirds, these timberlands give territories to species adjusted to colder environments. Relocation is normal among birds in these districts, with occasional developments to take advantage of changing asset accessibility.

Prairies and Savannas:
Open Prairies: Backing species like songbirds, pipits, and field sparrows. These territories are portrayed by a blend of grasses and dissipated bushes, giving reasonable circumstances to ground-settling birds.

Savannas: A momentary living space among backwoods and fields, facilitating various species, including raptors, bustards, and finches. Savannas exhibit a mosaic of trees, grasses, and open spaces.

Deserts:
Xeric Transformations: Birds in deserts, like roadrunners and songbirds, display variations to parched conditions. Specific bills, proficient water use, and ways of behaving like nighttime rummaging add to their endurance in unforgiving desert conditions.

B. Sea-going and Wetland Living spaces:
Freshwater Biological systems:

Lakes and Waterways: Living space for waterbirds like ducks, herons, and kingfishers. These birds use freshwater biological systems for rummaging, settling, and raising their young.

Wetlands: Basic living spaces for a different exhibit of waterbirds, including egrets, ibises, and rails. Wetlands give favorable places, taking care of regions, and visit locales for transitory species.

Marine Biological systems:
Beach front Natural surroundings: Seabirds, like gulls, terns, and gooney birds, possess waterfront regions. Rough bluffs, sandy shores, and seaward islands act as settling locales and scrounging grounds.

Open Seas: Pelagic seabirds, similar to shearwaters and petrels, burn through broadened periods over open seas, covering immense distances looking for food. They are all around adjusted to life on the wing and show ways of behaving like unique taking off.

C. Particular Living spaces:
Metropolitan Conditions:

Metropolitan Transformations: Some bird species have adjusted to metropolitan conditions, flourishing in nearness to human exercises. Pigeons, sparrows, and crows are instances of birds that have effectively adjusted to metropolitan scenes.

Settling on Designs: Birds might utilize structures, edges, and other human-made structures for settling. Swifts, swallows, and certain raptors are known for settling on tall designs.

Mountain Living spaces:
Snow capped Zones: High-height living spaces in precipitous districts support species adjusted to cold and brutal circumstances. Snow finches, ptarmigans, and falcons are instances of birds possessing high zones.

Montane Woodlands: Birds in montane backwoods, found at mid-rises, may incorporate species like trogons, thrushes, and flycatchers adjusted to the remarkable environmental states of bumpy landscape.

III. Environmental Meaning of Bird Natural surroundings
A. Biodiversity Areas of interest:
Certain locales all over the planet are perceived as biodiversity areas of interest because of their elevated degrees of species lavishness and endemism. Tropical rainforests, for instance, are biodiversity areas of interest where a large number of bird species coincide in complex biological systems.

B. Biological system Administrations:
Birds give vital biological system administrations, including fertilization, seed dispersal, and irritation control. Pollinators like hummingbirds and seed dispersers like frugivorous birds add to the conceptive achievement and recovery of plant species.

C. Marker Species:
Birds are frequently utilized as marks of natural wellbeing. Changes in bird populaces, ways of behaving, or conveyances can flag more extensive changes in environments. Observing bird species evaluates the effects of environmental change, natural surroundings misfortune, and contamination.

D. Ecotourism and Social Worth:
Birdwatching, a famous sporting action, adds to ecotourism. Many individuals travel to notice and value different bird species in their regular territories, supporting neighborhood economies and encouraging an association among individuals and nature.

IV. Protection Difficulties and Techniques
A. Natural surroundings Misfortune and Discontinuity:
Human exercises, including deforestation, urbanization, and horticulture, lead to living space misfortune and discontinuity, compromising bird populaces. Preservation procedures incorporate saving basic environments, laying out safeguarded regions, and advancing manageable land use.

B. Environmental Change:
Environmental change presents huge difficulties for birds by modifying temperature examples, precipitation, and the accessibility of assets. Preservation endeavors center around moderating environmental change influences, safeguarding transitory courses, and establishing environment tough living spaces.

C. Contamination:
Contamination, including pesticides, plastics, and oil slicks, adversely influences bird wellbeing and natural surroundings. Protection drives include lessening contamination, reestablishing tainted regions, and advancing manageable practices.

D. Obtrusive Species:
The presentation of non-local species upsets environments and postures dangers to local bird populaces. Protection endeavors focus on the control and destruction of obtrusive species, forestalling further natural lopsided characteristics.

E. Safeguarded Regions and Protection Stores:
Laying out and keeping up with safeguarded regions, public parks, and protection saves are essential for defending environments and giving asylums to bird species. Preservation techniques likewise include making availability between safeguarded regions.

F. Local area Commitment and Training:
Including nearby networks in protection endeavors encourages a feeling of obligation and advances maintainable practices. Training and mindfulness programs raise public cognizance about the significance of bird living spaces and the requirement for preservation.

1.3 Adaptations and Specializations in Different Bird Species

Birds, with their unbelievable variety, have developed a bunch of variations and specializations that empower them to flourish in different conditions and environmental specialties. From the smooth, smoothed out collections of raptors to the complicated plumage and romance presentations of warblers, every transformation is a demonstration of the developmental creativity of these padded miracles. This investigation digs into the surprising transformations and specializations tracked down in various bird species, exhibiting the assorted manners by which birds have molded their bodies, ways of behaving, and physiological attributes to overcome the difficulties of their surroundings.

I. Mouth and Bill Variety:
A. Flesh eating Specializations:

Raptors (Flying predators): Raptors, including birds, falcons, and hawks, have strong snared noses and sharp claws. These variations are particular for catching and consuming prey, exhibiting a dominant hunter's effectiveness in the avian world.

Owls: Nighttime trackers like owls have particular snouts intended for destroying their prey. Their quiet flight and facial circles help in finding and catching prey in low light circumstances.

B. Herbivorous Transformations:
Finches: Seed-eating birds like finches have adjusted noses for airing out seeds. The variety in bill shapes among finch species mirrors their capacity to take advantage of different kinds of seeds.

Parrots: Parrots, known for their dynamic plumage and knowledge, have solid, snared snouts adjusted for opening nuts and seeds. A few animal types, similar to the Kea parrot, even display device use in controlling items.

C. Nectar Taking care of Specializations:
Hummingbirds: Hummingbirds are portrayed by lengthy, specific bills and extendable, tube-like tongues adjusted for extricating nectar from blossoms. Their fast wing beats and abilities to drift make them productive pollinators.

Sunbirds: Tracked down in tropical locales, sunbirds likewise have long, thin bills for benefiting from nectar. Their luminous plumage adds to their appeal as pollinators in different biological systems.

II. Taking care of Procedures:
A. Insectivorous Ways of behaving:

Flycatchers: Birds like flycatchers display airborne aerobatic exhibition to get bugs in flight. Their wide bills and coordinated moves make them proficient at catching flying prey.

Woodpeckers: Specific scavenging ways of behaving are found in woodpeckers, furnished areas of strength for with and long, extensible tongues for extricating bugs from tree covering. Their drumming serves both for correspondence and finding stowed away prey.

B. Channel taking care of Specializations:
Flamingos: Channel feeders like flamingos utilize their interesting bills to separate little creatures, green growth, and spineless creatures from water bodies. The topsy turvy position of their bills takes into consideration effective channel taking care of.

Pelicans: Pelicans have long bills with an enormous gular pocket, empowering them to gather up fish and water and afterward channel the water prior to gulping the prey.

III. Physiological Variations:
A. Movement Systems:

Cold Tern: The Icy Tern holds the record for the longest transient excursion, venturing out from the Icy to the Antarctic and back. This species displays physiological variations for perseverance flight, including effective energy use and route capacities.

Bar-followed Godwit: This bird holds the record for the longest direct flight, covering huge number of kilometers during relocation. Physiological variations incorporate expanded muscle productivity and the capacity to shrivel interior organs to diminish weight.

B. High-height Variations:
Andean Condor: Tracked down in the Andes mountains, the Andean Condor exhibits variations to high-height flight. Enormous wings and effective taking off capacities permit these birds to explore the rugged landscape easily.

Snowfinches: Occupying elevated zones, snowfinches have adjusted to low-oxygen conditions by creating effective respiratory frameworks and specific hemoglobin for oxygen transport.

IV. Romance Presentations and Plumage:
A. Elaborate Romance Presentations:

Birds of Heaven: The extreme romance presentations of birds of heaven, like the Wilson's Bird of Heaven, include dynamic plumage, perplexing moves, and novel vocalizations. These presentations are critical for mate fascination.

Bowerbirds: Male bowerbirds fabricate many-sided nooks and brighten them with vivid items to draw in females. The intricacy of the grove and the male's showcases impact female mate decision.

B. Shading and Cover:
Peafowl: The bright plumage of male peafowls, especially the glowing tail feathers, fills in as a visual presentation during romance. The dynamic tones draw in females, displaying the significance of visual signs in mate choice.

Ptarmigan: interestingly, species like the ptarmigan show occasional hue changes for disguise. In winter, their plumage becomes white to mix with the frigid environmental elements, giving viable disguise from hunters.

Chapter 2
Ecosystem Services Provided by Birds

Birds, with their different species and wonderful transformations, assume a pivotal part in giving an extensive variety of environment administrations. From fertilization and seed dispersal to bother control and supplement cycling, birds contribute fundamentally to the working and strength of environments around the world. This complete investigation expects to disentangle the mind boggling trap of biological system administrations given by birds, displaying their irreplaceable job in keeping up with environmental equilibrium and biodiversity.

I. Fertilization Administrations:
A. Job of Pollinators:

Significance of Fertilization: Many bird species act as pollinators, moving dust between blossoms as they search for nectar. This interaction is crucial for the proliferation of blooming plants, adding to the development of products of the soil.

Hummingbirds as Pollinators: Hummingbirds, with their specific bills and novel abilities to float, are effective pollinators. They are drawn to splendidly shaded, cylindrical blossoms, and their long bills work with admittance to nectar, guaranteeing powerful fertilization.

B. Bird-Pollinated Plants:
Tropical Orchids: Orchids, particularly those in tropical areas, frequently depend on unambiguous bird species for fertilization. The intricate shapes and shades of orchid blossoms are transformations to draw specifically bird pollinators.

Bird of Heaven Plants: The complicated and conspicuous blossoms of the Bird of Heaven plant are intended to draw in unambiguous bird pollinators. The remarkable construction of the blossom works with the exchange of dust during taking care of.

II. Seed Dispersal:
A. Significance of Seed Dispersal:

Variety of Seed Dispersal Methodologies: Birds add to seed dispersal by consuming foods grown from the ground discharging the seeds in various areas. This dispersal component improves plant colonization, hereditary variety, and the foundation of new populaces.

Endozoochory and Epizoochory: Birds take part in both endozoochory (inner vehicle of seeds inside the stomach related framework) and epizoochory (outer vehicle of seeds joined to quills or feet). This double methodology adds to the outcome of different plant species.

B. Instances of Bird-Intervened Seed Dispersal:
Fruigivorous Birds: Species like toucans, hornbills, and frugivorous pigeons assume a vital part in seed dispersal. They consume foods grown from the ground seeds in various areas, adding to the recovery of plant networks.

Imperiled Plant Species: Some plant species, particularly those with enormous seeds, rely upon explicit bird species for dispersal. Preservation endeavors frequently center around safeguarding both the plants and the birds to guarantee shared endurance.

III. Bother Control:
A. Insectivorous Birds:

Normal Hunters of Bugs: Many bird species are ravenous insectivores, going after a large number of bugs. This predation helps control bug populaces, forestalling flare-ups that could adversely affect yields and vegetation.

Farming Advantages: Birds, like swallows, flycatchers, and larks, add to bother control in rural scenes. They assist ranchers with decreasing the requirement for compound pesticides, advancing reasonable and eco-accommodating cultivating rehearses.

B. Job of Raptors:
Top Hunters in Environments: Raptors, including owls, falcons, and birds, possess the head of the avian pecking order. Their predation on rodents and little warm blooded creatures keeps an equilibrium in prey populaces, forestalling overgrazing and environment corruption.

Stable Owls in Farming: Animal dwellingplace owls are prestigious for their rat hunting capacities. Ranchers frequently energize the presence of animal dwellingplace owls in horticultural regions to control populaces of mice and rodents, decreasing harvest harm.

IV. Supplement Cycling:
A. Commitment to Decay:

Rummaging Birds: Searching birds, like vultures and crows, assume a basic part in supplement cycling. They consume carcass, speeding up the deterioration cycle and returning supplements to the dirt.

Social Biological system Administrations: In certain societies, rummaging birds are viewed as significant for their part in tidying up corpses. This social biological system administration improves human prosperity by keeping a spotless and sound climate.

B. Guano as Compost:
Seabird Provinces: Seabirds, similar to guillemots and gulls, structure huge states on seaside precipices and islands. The collection of their droppings, known as guano, is wealthy in supplements and fills in as a characteristic compost for encompassing environments.

Authentic Significance: Guano was generally dug for rural use because of its high phosphorus and nitrogen content. The presence of seabird settlements subsequently adds to both nearby and worldwide supplement cycling.

V. Guideline of Plant Populaces:
A. Influence on Vegetation Elements:

Herbivorous Birds: Some bird species assume a part in controlling plant populaces by consuming seeds, seedlings, or vegetation. This herbivory helps shape the design and sythesis of plant networks.

Island Environments: In island biological systems, where plants might confront restricted herbivory, the presentation of herbivorous birds can impact the successional cycles and elements of plant networks.

VI. Social and Sporting Qualities:
A. Ecotourism and Birdwatching:
Monetary Commitments: Birds draw in ecotourists and birdwatchers, adding to neighborhood economies.

The presence of different bird species in normal territories upgrades the stylish worth of these areas.

Instructive Open doors: Birdwatching gives instructive open doors and cultivates an association among individuals and nature. This social environment administration advances mindfulness and preservation endeavors.

B. Representative and Tasteful Worth:

Public Images: Birds frequently act as public images, reflecting social personality and values. Models incorporate the bald eagle as an image of the US and the kiwi as an image of New Zealand.

Tasteful Appreciation: Birds, with their changed plumage, melodies, and ways of behaving, add to the stylish enthusiasm for regular scenes. Their presence improves the general excellence of biological systems.

VII. Environment Guideline:
A. Carbon Sequestration:

Woods Birds: Birds possessing backwoods add to carbon sequestration by impacting vegetation elements. The presence of seed-scattering birds upholds the recovery of woods, which go about as carbon sinks.

Mangrove Environments: Seaside birds, like herons and shorebirds, add to carbon sequestration in mangrove biological systems. Their exercises upgrade the wellbeing and flexibility of these fundamental seaside territories.

B. Environment Responsive Ways of behaving:

Relocation Examples: Bird movement designs are frequently impacted by environment conditions. Changes in environment can influence the timing and courses of movement, featuring the interconnectedness between bird conduct and environment guideline.

Pointer Species: Birds are viewed as marker species for environmental change influences. Changes in dissemination, changes in rearing seasons, and modifications in transitory examples act as early advance notice indications of environment related disturbances.

VIII. Difficulties and Preservation Concerns:
A. Living space Misfortune and Fracture:

Urbanization and Agribusiness: The development of metropolitan regions and horticultural exercises prompts environment misfortune and fracture, influencing bird populaces and their capacity to give biological system administrations.

Preservation Systems: Protection endeavors should zero in on safeguarding and reestablishing assorted natural surroundings, making untamed life halls, and executing maintainable land use practices to relieve the impacts of living space misfortune.

B. Environmental Change Effects:
Modified Relocation Examples: Environmental change can upset conventional movement courses and timing, influencing the capacity of transitory birds to give fertilization and seed dispersal administrations.

Variation Systems: Preservation methodologies incorporate establishing environment strong living spaces, safeguarding visit locales along movement courses, and observing changes in bird ways of behaving connected with environment shifts.

C. Contamination and Foreign substances:
Pesticides and Synthetics: The utilization of pesticides and synthetics in farming postures dangers to birds, especially those associated with bug control administrations. Contamination from foreign substances can hurt both individual birds and whole populaces.

Backing for Feasible Practices: Protection drives should advocate for economical rural practices, lessen the utilization of unsafe synthetic substances, and advance mindfulness about the effects of contamination on bird populaces.

D. Obtrusive Species and Contending Interests:
Disturbance of Environment Elements: The presentation of intrusive species can upset biological system elements, influencing both bird populaces and the administrations they give. Contending interests, like obtrusive plants, can modify territories and effect bird conduct.

Incorporated Vermin The board: Coordinated bother the executives methodologies, which think about the job of birds as regular bug regulators, can assist with finding some kind of harmony between agrarian requirements and biodiversity protection.

IX. Preservation Methodologies and Feasible Practices:
A. Safeguarded Regions and Stores:

Foundation of Safeguarded Regions: Making and keeping up with safeguarded regions and untamed life saves are fundamental for defending natural surroundings basic to bird populaces. These regions act as safe-havens for rearing, scrounging, and settling.

Passageway Network: Laying out untamed life halls between safeguarded regions works with the development of birds, especially transitory species. Passageway network upgrades hereditary variety and supports environmental cycles.

B. Living space Reclamation and Upgrade:
Reforestation and Wetland Reclamation: Living space rebuilding drives center around replanting local vegetation, reforesting corrupted regions, and reestablishing wetlands. These endeavors give fundamental living spaces to assorted bird species.

Metropolitan Green Spaces: Making and keeping up with green spaces in metropolitan conditions improves environments for birds adjusted to metropolitan settings. Metropolitan parks, green rooftops, and local area gardens add to metropolitan biodiversity.

C. Exploration and Checking Projects:
Long haul Observing: Executing long haul checking programs is essential for following bird populaces, grasping their ways of behaving, and recognizing likely dangers. Research adds to confirm based preservation procedures.

Mechanical Progressions: The utilization of innovation, like satellite following, radio telemetry, and resident science drives, improves the capacity to screen bird developments, movement examples, and reactions to ecological changes.

D. Local area Commitment and Instruction:
Nearby Support: Including neighborhood networks in bird protection endeavors encourages a feeling of stewardship. Drawing in networks in birdwatching, living space rebuilding, and instructive projects fortifies the association among individuals and nature.

Schooling on Environment Administrations: Bringing issues to light about the biological system administrations given by birds is fundamental.

Training programs feature the significance of birds in keeping up with environmental equilibrium and advance preservation activities.

E. Worldwide Joint effort:
Transient Bird Preservation Arrangements: Cooperative endeavors between nations are fundamental for the protection of transitory bird species. Peaceful accords, for example, the Transitory Bird Deal Act, mean to safeguard birds that cross numerous locales.

Shared Liability: Perceiving the common obligation regarding bird preservation supports worldwide joint effort. Joint drives address transboundary dangers, guaranteeing the prosperity of bird populaces across assorted scenes.

2.1   Pollination by Birds

Fertilization by birds, known as ornithophily, is a captivating and critical environmental cycle that assumes a huge part in the propagation of many plant species. While bugs are in many cases the main organic entities that strike a chord while pondering fertilization, birds likewise contribute essentially to this imperative biological system administration. The coevolution of blooming plants and birds has prompted a momentous variety of bird-pollinated blossoms, each adjusted to draw in and work with fertilization by these avian guests.

One of the most particular elements of bird-pollinated plants is their dynamic and prominent blossoms. Dissimilar to numerous bug pollinated blossoms that frequently depend on aroma to draw in pollinators, bird-pollinated blossoms will generally be brilliantly hued, with shades of red, orange, and pink being especially normal. This is on the grounds that birds, particularly hummingbirds, have a fantastic feeling of variety vision, and these strong tints act as visual signs to draw in them. The rounded state of many bird-pollinated blossoms is another transformation, giving a helpful construction to the long bills of birds to arrive at nectar profound inside the bloom.

Hummingbirds are among the most notable bird pollinators, and they are particularly capable at benefiting from nectar from cylindrical blossoms. Their long, specific bills and extendable, tube-like tongues permit them to get to nectar concealed profound inside the flower tubes. As they feed, their heads come into contact with the regenerative pieces of the blossom, moving dust starting with one sprout then onto the next. This mutualistic relationship benefits the two players — the plant gets proficient fertilization administrations, while the bird gets a rich wellspring of energy from the nectar.

Aside from hummingbirds, other bird species likewise add to fertilization. Sunbirds, found in locales like Africa and Asia, are referred to for their job as pollinators, especially in tropical environments.

Their thin bills and brush-tipped tongues are adjusted for extricating nectar from different blossoms. At times, blossoms have developed to match the bill lengths of explicit bird species, guaranteeing an exact fit and improving the probability of effective fertilization.

One wonderful illustration of bird-pollinated plants is the gathering of orchids known as the "bird orchids" (Disa species) tracked down in South Africa. These orchids mirror the presence of birds, with particular designs that look like the heads of sunbirds. The duplicity is persuading to such an extent that male sunbirds are drawn to these blossoms, endeavoring to mate with the orchid's designs, and all the while, they accidentally move dust between blossoms.

The job of bird fertilization reaches out past style and environmental interest; it is vital for the propagation of many plant species. A few plants have developed to be on the whole subject to bird fertilization, and interruptions to this interaction can have huge ramifications for their endurance. Furthermore, the geological appropriation of bird-pollinated plants frequently lines up with the scopes of their avian pollinators, underscoring the significance of these cooperations in molding biological systems. While bird fertilization is a productive and fruitful procedure for some plants, it accompanies difficulties. Birds are exceptionally versatile, and their searching examples can be impacted by different elements, including food accessibility and occasional changes. This fluctuation can influence the consistency of fertilization administrations for plant species depending on birds. Also, territory misfortune and environmental change can upset the sensitive equilibrium of these mutualistic connections, presenting dangers to both the plants and their avian pollinators.

2.2   Seed Dispersal and Forest Regeneration

Seed dispersal is a basic biological cycle that assumes a fundamental part in the recovery and manageability of woodlands. It is an instrument by which plants guarantee the spread of their seeds to new areas, adding to hereditary variety and empowering the foundation of new people. Different specialists, including wind, water, creatures, and even people, take part in seed dispersal, each with its one of a kind systems and outcomes. With regards to woodland biological systems, the course of seed dispersal is unpredictably connected to the recovery and in general strength of these essential living spaces.

Wind Dispersal:

One of the most widely recognized components of seed dispersal in woodlands is through the breeze. Many trees, like maple, debris, and pine, produce seeds with particular variations for wind dispersal.

These transformations frequently incorporate wings or a parachute-like construction that permits the seed to be conveyed by the breeze over impressive distances. Wind dispersal is especially viable in open natural surroundings, like glades and clearings inside backwoods, where seeds can travel unhindered.

As well as supporting the colonization of new regions, wind dispersal likewise adds to the spatial dissemination of plant species inside a backwoods. Various types of trees might have seeds that are adjusted to travel differing distances on the breeze, prompting unmistakable examples of seed affidavit. Over the long run, this can bring about the foundation of various tree species at various good ways from the parent trees, adding to the improvement of timberland construction and structure.

Creature Dispersal:

Creatures, the two vertebrates and spineless creatures, assume a significant part in seed dispersal inside timberland environments. Birds, well evolved creatures, bugs, and even reptiles add to this cycle, frequently accidentally as they consume natural products or seeds. Many plants have developed to deliver organic products that are alluring to creatures, captivating them to eat the foods grown from the ground store the seeds in new areas through their excrement.

Birds, for instance, can be viable seed dispersers, particularly for little seeds that stick to their quills or are discharged after ingestion. Bigger vertebrates, like bears and deer, may scatter seeds via conveying them on their fur or hooves. Rodents and little warm blooded creatures assume a huge part too, frequently storing seeds for later utilization and unexpectedly helping with the dispersal of those they neglect to recover.

One captivating illustration of creature helped seed dispersal is the myrmecochory, a mutualistic connection between specific plants and subterranean insects. Seeds of such plants commonly have a greasy extremity called an elaiosome, which draws in subterranean insects. The subterranean insects convey the seeds back to their homes, consume the elaiosome, and dispose of the seed in a supplement rich climate, frequently making an ideal germination site.

Water Dispersal:

In riparian regions and wetland biological systems, water fills in as a powerful specialist for seed dispersal. A few plants produce seeds that float and are adjusted to get by in sea-going conditions. These seeds can be conveyed by water ebbs and flows, working with their spread downstream or across water bodies. Moreover, water-scattered seeds might be ingested by sea-going creatures, adding to dispersal through their stomach related frameworks.

Water dispersal is especially fundamental for the recovery of plant species in regions inclined to occasional flooding. It permits seeds to arrive at new places where they can develop and set up a good foundation for themselves when floodwaters subside.

This component is critical for keeping up with biodiversity in riparian biological systems and adds to the versatility of plant networks in unique conditions.

Woods Recovery:
The course of seed dispersal is firmly connected to backwoods recovery, which alludes to the restoration and restoration of woodland biological systems over the long haul. Without compelling seed dispersal, the capacity of timberlands to recover and recuperate from aggravations like out of control fires, logging, or infection would be seriously compromised.
Compelling seed dispersal advances hereditary variety inside timberland populaces. As seeds are moved away from parent trees, they have the potential chance to develop and fill in new conditions. This variety is fundamental for the flexibility of woods biological systems, as it improves the probability that a few people inside the populace will be adjusted to changing natural circumstances, like changes in environment or the presence of new nuisances.
The spatial examples of seed statement coming about because of various dispersal instruments additionally add to the construction and sythesis of woods. Wind-scattered seeds, for instance, may prompt an all the more even conveyance of tree species, while creature scattered seeds might bring about bunches of trees around preferred taking care of or settling locales. These examples add to the intricacy and biodiversity of woodland environments.

In upset regions, for example, those impacted by logging or catastrophic events, the job of seed dispersal turns out to be especially significant. Trailblazer species, frequently described by seeds that are effectively scattered and fast to sprout, assume a crucial part in the beginning phases of backwoods recovery. These species assist with balancing out the dirt, give conceal, and make microenvironments helpful for the foundation of other, frequently more slow developing, tree species.

Difficulties to Seed Dispersal and Woods Recovery:
Human exercises, including deforestation, urbanization, and the presentation of intrusive species, can present critical difficulties to seed dispersal and woodland recovery. Discontinuity of normal living spaces can restrict the development of creatures that assume a part in seed dispersal, upsetting laid out designs and thwarting the recovery of timberlands. Intrusive species may outcompete local plants or upset mutualistic connections among plants and their dispersers, further influencing the normal cycles of woodland recovery.
Environmental change additionally presents difficulties to seed dispersal and woods recovery.

Adjusted precipitation designs, temperature systems, and the recurrence and force of outrageous climate occasions can influence the timing and progress of seed germination, seedling foundation, and generally speaking backwoods recovery. Some tree species might find it trying to distribute their seeds to reasonable microenvironments as environment conditions shift, prompting potential jumbles between seed appropriation and ideal germination destinations.

Preservation Suggestions:
Understanding the systems and significance of seed dispersal in timberland environments has huge ramifications for preservation endeavors. Preservation systems ought to expect to safeguard and reestablish the regular cycles of seed dispersal, permitting woodlands to recover and adjust to evolving conditions. This might include safeguarding natural surroundings availability, overseeing obtrusive species, and relieving the effects of environmental change.
Endeavors to save and reestablish woods ought to likewise consider the significance of keeping up with different arrays of creature species that add to seed dispersal. Protection of key seed-scattering creatures, including birds, vertebrates, and bugs, is fundamental for guaranteeing the proceeded with wellbeing and flexibility of backwoods environments. Safeguarding the territories and movement halls of these creatures contributes not exclusively to their endurance yet additionally to the biological administrations they give.

2.3   Pest Control and Ecological Balance
Bug control is a complicated and multi-layered part of horticulture and environment the executives. It includes the administration of life forms that present dangers to harvests, domesticated animals, or human wellbeing. While the prompt objective of irritation control is to limit financial misfortunes and defend human prosperity, moving toward these mediations with a comprehension of their more extensive environmental implications is pivotal. Offsetting powerful bug control with the protection of environmental concordance is fundamental for keeping up with biodiversity, biological system flexibility, and maintainable farming practices.

Sorts of Nuisances:
Vermin are life forms that can hurt or impede human exercises, especially in farming. They can incorporate bugs, rodents, growths, microorganisms, infections, and, surprisingly, bigger creatures like deer or birds. These living beings can possibly harm crops, send illnesses, or contend with people for assets. The variety of nuisances and their capacity to adjust to changing circumstances make bother control a steady test.

Synthetic Bug Control:
By and large, synthetic pesticides have been an essential device in bother control systems. These manufactured synthetics are intended to target and wipe out bugs, giving a speedy and frequently viable answer for bother invasions. Nonetheless, the utilization of synthetic pesticides raises critical biological worries. Aimless application can hurt non-target species, including helpful bugs, soil microorganisms, and sea-going life. Pesticide deposits may likewise continue in the climate, influencing environments long after application.
Also, the rehashed utilization of synthetic pesticides can prompt the improvement of obstruction in bother populaces. After some time, bugs might advance to endure the impacts of these synthetic compounds, delivering them less powerful and requiring the improvement of new, possibly more strong pesticides. This cycle adds to a persistent weapons contest among vermin and nuisance control strategies.

Natural Irritation Control:
Perceiving the restrictions and ecological effects of compound pesticides, natural nuisance control has acquired unmistakable quality as a more feasible other option. This approach includes the utilization of normal adversaries, like hunters, parasites, and microbes, to control bug populaces. For instance, presenting or upgrading populaces of gainful bugs like ladybugs or parasitoid wasps can assist with overseeing irritation bugs in agribusiness.
Organic control strategies influence the biological connections between species, meaning to make an equilibrium that favors normal nuisance concealment. This approach is much of the time more particular, focusing on unambiguous irritations while limiting damage to non-target living beings. It additionally will in general be more practical in the long haul, as it depends on the natural elements of the climate.

Coordinated Irritation The board (IPM):
Coordinated Irritation The board (IPM) addresses a comprehensive methodology that joins different vermin control strategies to accomplish successful and economical nuisance the executives. IPM coordinates organic, social, physical, and synthetic control procedures to limit the monetary, wellbeing, and ecological dangers related with bother the executives.
Social practices inside IPM include altering agrarian practices to decrease the weakness of yields to bugs. Crop pivot, polyculture (developing various harvests together), and the utilization of irritation safe assortments are instances of social methodologies. These techniques center around establishing conditions less helpful for bother improvement.

Actual control techniques incorporate the utilization of hindrances, traps, and other actual means to keep bothers from arriving at crops or to decrease their populaces. This can incorporate the utilization of nets, walls, and mechanical gadgets that actually block or catch bothers.

The joining of different control techniques in IPM considers a more nuanced and reasonable way to deal with bug the board. By joining procedures, ranchers can diminish their dependence on compound pesticides, limit ecological effects, and upgrade the general flexibility of agroecosystems.

Natural Equilibrium and Biodiversity:

Keeping up with natural equilibrium is key to the drawn out wellbeing and manageability of environments. Biodiversity, the assortment of life in a specific natural surroundings or environment, assumes a urgent part in this equilibrium. Every species in an environment adds to its working, and the connections between species assist with managing populaces and keep up with harmony.

Bother control techniques, especially those that include substance pesticides, can possibly disturb biological equilibrium by affecting non-target species. For instance, the decay of pollinator populaces because of pesticide use can have flowing impacts on plant propagation and the whole environment's wellbeing. Essentially, the end of normal hunters can prompt an expansion in bug populaces, making a pattern of reliance on compound mediations.

Interestingly, natural vermin control and coordinated bother the board focus on biological equilibrium. By utilizing regular foes and integrating an assortment of control strategies, these methodologies work inside the current natural structure. Gainful bugs, for example, add to bug concealment, and the assorted procedures utilized in IPM assist with forestalling the improvement of obstruction and keep up with the wellbeing of the biological system.

Difficulties and Contemplations:

While the standards of incorporated bother the board and organic control are promising, their broad reception faces difficulties. Ranchers frequently experience monetary tensions, and the forthright expenses or potential dangers related with elective vermin control techniques can be boundaries to reception. Schooling and effort are vital parts of advancing these manageable works on, assisting ranchers with grasping the drawn out advantages and supporting their progress to additional biological methodologies. Globalization and the development of merchandise and individuals likewise add to the spread of irritations and sicknesses. Obtrusive species, which might need regular hunters in their new surroundings, can immediately become bothers and disturb neighborhood environments.

Successful irritation the executives procedures should consider these more extensive environmental and worldwide elements to address the interconnected idea of biological systems.

Moreover, environmental change brings extra vulnerabilities into bug the board. Changed temperature and precipitation examples can impact the circulation and conduct of nuisances, possibly requiring changes in charge techniques. Versatile and adaptable methodologies are vital for address the difficulties presented by an evolving environment.

Supportable Agribusiness and Nuisance The board:

The idea of economical horticulture accentuates the significance of practices that help the drawn out wellbeing of biological systems, soil, and networks. Feasible nuisance the board lines up with these standards by trying to adjust the necessities of agribusiness with ecological stewardship. Agroecology, a methodology that incorporates natural standards into farming frameworks, offers a structure for creating supportable vermin the board systems.

Agroecological rehearses center around upgrading biodiversity, building soil wellbeing, and encouraging tough biological systems. These practices frequently include the utilization of cover crops, crop revolutions, and agroforestry to make assorted and stable agroecosystems. By supporting sound soils and advancing assorted territories, these methodologies add to regular vermin guideline and decrease the dependence on outside inputs.

Crop broadening is one more key procedure in feasible horticulture and nuisance the executives. Establishing various yields decreases the gamble of bug episodes since bothers that represent considerable authority in one harvest are more averse to cause broad harm. Furthermore, different editing frameworks add to a stronger and versatile horticultural scene.

2.4   Nutrient Cycling and Soil Health

Supplement cycling is a principal natural interaction that assumes a critical part in keeping up with soil wellbeing and supporting the efficiency of earthly biological systems. It includes the constant development and reusing of fundamental supplements like nitrogen, phosphorus, potassium, carbon, and others between the dirt, plants, and different creatures. This many-sided dance of supplements is essential for the development of plants, the soundness of biological systems, and at last, the prosperity of all life on The planet.

The Supplement Cycle:

The supplement cycle is a unique framework wherein supplements travel through different stages, progressing between residing creatures, the dirt, and the environment.

The cycle ordinarily includes four principal processes: take-up by plants, utilization by herbivores, decay of natural matter, and mineralization of supplements once again into the dirt.

Plants assume a focal part in supplement cycling by retaining supplements from the dirt through their underlying foundations. These supplements are then used for different physiological cycles, like development, propagation, and protection systems. At the point when plants are devoured by herbivores, the supplements are moved up the established pecking order. Disintegration of plant and creature stays by microorganisms, like microbes and parasites, discharges natural matter once again into the dirt, finishing the supplement cycle.

Microorganisms and Disintegration:

Microorganisms, especially microbes and organisms, are vital participants in the decay phase of the supplement cycle. They separate complex natural matter into more straightforward structures, delivering supplements in a structure that plants can retain. This interaction reuses supplements as well as adds to the development of humus, a dim, natural part of soil that works on its construction, water maintenance, and supplement holding limit.

The productivity of supplement cycling is impacted by the variety and movement of soil microorganisms. Solid soil overflowing with an assortment of microbial life adds to strong supplement cycling, cultivating the accessibility of fundamental components for plant development. Thus, plants support these microorganisms by furnishing them with natural mixtures through root exudates, framing a cooperative relationship that upgrades soil wellbeing.

Soil Construction and Ripeness:

Supplement cycling assumes an essential part in keeping up with soil design and ripeness. As natural matter disintegrates, it adds to the arrangement of soil totals, which are groups of soil particles bound together. These totals make pore spaces in the dirt, further developing air circulation, water penetration, and root entrance. A very much organized soil gives an optimal climate to establish roots to get to supplements and water, advancing sound plant development.

Besides, supplement cycling impacts soil richness by directing the accessibility of fundamental supplements. At the point when natural matter deteriorates, it discharges supplements like nitrogen, phosphorus, and potassium into the dirt. The persistent cycling of these supplements guarantees that they stay accessible for plants, forestalling supplement exhaustion and supporting soil richness after some time.

Human Effect on Supplement Cycling:
Human exercises, like farming and urbanization, can fundamentally affect supplement cycling and soil wellbeing. Serious cultivating rehearses frequently include the utilization of engineered composts, which can upset normal supplement cycles. While these manures can give a fast increase in supplements to crops, they may likewise prompt supplement lopsided characteristics, soil fermentation, and long haul debasement of soil wellbeing.
Unnecessary utilization of composts, especially nitrogen-based manures, can bring about supplement overflow into water bodies, causing water contamination and eutrophication. The disturbance of supplement cycles in amphibian biological systems can adversely affect water quality, sea-going life, and, surprisingly, human wellbeing. Deforestation and land-use changes related with metropolitan improvement likewise upset supplement cycling. The evacuation of vegetation dispenses with the contribution of natural matter into the dirt, diminishing microbial movement and supplement cycling. This disturbance can prompt soil disintegration, loss of soil richness, and expanded weakness to outrageous climate occasions.

Maintainable Practices for Soil Wellbeing:
Advancing economical practices is fundamental for protecting supplement cycling and keeping up with soil wellbeing. Crop turn, cover editing, and agroforestry are instances of practices that add to better soils. These methodologies upgrade biodiversity, further develop soil structure, and advance the proficient cycling of supplements.
Lessening dependence on engineered manures and consolidating natural revisions, like fertilizer and excrement, can assist with renewing soil natural matter and backing supplement cycling. Also, rehearsing insignificant culturing or no-work agribusiness assists save with dirtying structure and lessen unsettling influences that can disturb supplement cycling.
Preservation rehearses, for example, reforestation and the security of normal biological systems, assume a critical part in keeping up with the equilibrium of supplement cycles. Timberlands, specifically, are skilled at supplement cycling, and their protection supports soil wellbeing for a bigger scope.

Chapter 3
Birds as Indicators of Environmental Health

Birds, with their different species and broad conveyance, act as important marks of natural wellbeing. Their aversion to changes in environments, ways of behaving, and physiology makes them successful gauges of the general prosperity of natural surroundings. As sentinel species, birds offer significant experiences into the effects of natural stressors, going from contamination and living space misfortune to environmental change. This far reaching investigation will dive into the meaning of birds as marks of natural wellbeing, analyzing the different manners by which avian populaces mirror the condition of the climate and the ramifications for more extensive biological frameworks.

I. Presentation

Birds have for quite some time been perceived as bioindicators, species whose presence, overflow, conduct, or physiology can give bits of knowledge into the environmental states of their territories. Their nearby relationship with different conditions, going from woods and wetlands to metropolitan regions, positions birds as delicate responders to changes in these biological systems. This responsiveness is credited to their dependence on unambiguous assets, like food, water, and appropriate settling locales, and their capacity to adjust to natural varieties.

II. Bird Species as Pointers
A. Natural surroundings Explicitness and Inclinations

Different bird species show changing levels of environment particularity, with some being exceptionally specific and others more versatile. This reach permits researchers to evaluate the soundness of explicit environments in light of the presence or nonappearance of specific bird species. For instance, the presence of specific bird species, for example, the Seen Owl in old-development woods, can demonstrate the environmental honesty of these living spaces.

B. Marker Species for Contamination

Birds are especially delicate to natural contaminations, making them astounding marks of contamination levels. Seabirds, for example, can aggregate toxins from marine conditions in their tissues.

Checking the centralizations of weighty metals, pesticides, or different toxins in bird tissues can give data about the degree of contamination in unambiguous biological systems.

C. Environmental Change Pointers

Changes in environment designs significantly affect bird conduct, relocation, and dissemination. Ornithologists and scientists use bird species as pointers to follow shifts in ranges, modified movement timings, and changes in reproducing designs. These markers contribute important information to the comprehension of more extensive environmental change influences on biological systems.

D. Conduct and Regenerative Achievement

Noticing the way of behaving and regenerative progress of bird populaces gives experiences into the general wellbeing of environments. Changes in settling achievement, taking care of conduct, or romance customs can demonstrate disturbances in the accessibility of food, adjustments in favorable places, or the effect of poisons on regenerative abilities.

III. Observing Methods

A. Bird Reviews and Enumeration Information

Orderly bird overviews and evaluation information, for example, those led by resident researchers and expert ornithologists, offer an abundance of data about bird populaces. These studies track changes in overflow, dissemination, and variety after some time, giving a benchmark to surveying ecological wellbeing.

B. Bird Banding and Following

Banding and following individual birds offer bits of knowledge into relocation designs, living space usage, and the general developments of bird populaces. This data is vital for figuring out the availability of environments and the effect of unsettling influences on bird conduct.

C. Bioacoustics Checking

Bird vocalizations, or bioacoustics, can be utilized to screen bird populaces. Changes in the recurrence, force, or variety of bird calls can show shifts in living space quality, populace thickness, or the presence of stressors.

D. Home Observing

Observing bird homes gives data on conceptive achievement and the effects of ecological variables on reproducing results. Home observing projects add to grasping the strength of bird populaces to evolving conditions.

IV. Instances of Bird Species as Markers
A. Bald Eagles (Haliaeetus leucocephalus)
The recuperation of Bald Eagle populaces in North America has been a commended example of overcoming adversity and a demonstration of the viability of preservation endeavors. Once recorded as jeopardized because of natural surroundings misfortune, contamination, and pesticide openness (explicitly DDT), the restriction on DDT and preservation measures have prompted the resurgence of Bald Eagles. Observing the wellbeing and regenerative outcome of these raptors gives experiences into the recuperation of oceanic biological systems and the progress of ecological guidelines.

B. Canaries in the Coal Mineshaft: Warblers as Contamination Markers
By and large, excavators utilized canaries to recognize harmful gases in coal mineshafts. Likewise, warblers in metropolitan and modern regions can act as signs of air and soil contamination. Studies have shown connections between's progressions in warbler populaces and the presence of toxins, making them important sentinels for metropolitan ecological quality.

C. Penguins in Antarctica
Penguin populaces in Antarctica and encompassing islands are touchy marks of environmental change. Changes in ocean ice conditions, temperature, and food accessibility influence penguins straightforwardly. Checking these alluring species assists researchers with understanding the natural outcomes of environmental change in quite possibly of the most immaculate and distant locale on The planet.

D. Seabirds and Plastic Contamination
Seabirds, with their rummaging conduct adrift, are especially defenseless to plastic contamination. Checking the ingestion of plastics via seabirds assists analysts with measuring the degree of marine contamination. The presence and wealth of plastics in the stomachs of seabirds give important information on the soundness of marine environments.

V. Difficulties and Contemplations
A. Complex Communications in Environments
While birds offer significant bits of knowledge into natural wellbeing, perceiving the intricacy of environmental systems is fundamental. Communications between species, territory elements, and the impact of numerous stressors can entangle the translation of bird information. An all encompassing comprehension of biological systems requires thinking about the more extensive setting of natural connections.

B. Various Stressors Affecting Birds

Birds frequently face various stressors at the same time, including environment misfortune, environmental change, contamination, and obtrusive species. Recognizing the particular effects of every stressor and understanding their synergistic impacts are continuous difficulties in natural exploration.

C. Spatial and Transient Fluctuation

Ecological circumstances can change spatially and transiently, presenting difficulties in laying out predictable benchmark information. Long haul observing and the incorporation of information from different locales are important to represent these varieties and give a more thorough comprehension of ecological wellbeing.

VI. Preservation Suggestions

A. Designated Preservation Measures

Involving birds as markers takes into account designated preservation measures. By understanding the particular requirements and reactions of bird species to ecological changes, preservation endeavors can be custom fitted to resolve the most major problems influencing environments.

B. Public Commitment and Instruction

Including the general population in bird observing projects contributes significant information as well as encourages natural mindfulness. Resident science drives, for example, birdwatching and cooperation in bird studies, interface individuals to their nearby environments and advance a feeling of stewardship.

C. Versatile Administration Systems

The unique idea of environments requires versatile administration systems. Constant checking of bird populaces empowers researchers and traditionalists to adjust methodologies in view of developing natural circumstances, guaranteeing the viability of protection endeavors.

3.1 Sensitivity of Birds to Environmental Changes

Birds, as exceptionally responsive and versatile animals, act as delicate marks of natural changes. Their ways of behaving, natural surroundings, and populaces reflect adjustments in environments brought about by human exercises, environmental change, living space misfortune, and contamination. This responsiveness is a demonstration of the multifaceted associations between avian species and their surroundings. In this investigation, we will dive into the different elements of bird aversion to natural changes, looking at social, physiological, and biological reactions that make birds urgent sentinels of ecological wellbeing.

II. Social Reactions
A. Movement Examples
Birds are prestigious for their transient ability, undertaking long excursions across landmasses looking for appropriate reproducing and taking care of grounds. Changes in relocation designs are among the most apparent signs of ecological movements. Modifications in temperature, asset accessibility, and living space conditions impact the timing and courses of relocation. Ornithologists track these progressions to comprehend the effect of environmental change on bird populaces.

For instance, studies have reported shifts in the planning of bird movement, for certain species showing up at favorable places prior or later than expected. These progressions line up with shifts in temperature and the accessibility of food assets. For example, hotter temperatures might prompt prior spring beginning, impacting the planning of bug development, an essential food hotspot for the vast majority transitory birds.

B. Changes in Searching Way of behaving
Birds show surprising flexibility in their rummaging ways of behaving, changing their taking care of procedures in light of natural changes. Changes in prey accessibility, driven by environment varieties or adjustments in vegetation structure, can provoke shifts in the scavenging conduct of bird species. Some might change to elective food sources, change rummaging areas, or adjust taking care of procedures.

For example, studies have noticed changes in the scavenging conduct of seabirds in light of adjustments in marine biological systems. Changes in fish conveyance because of environment driven changes in sea flows influence the accessibility of prey for seabirds. Thusly, seabirds might travel more noteworthy distances looking for food, influencing their energy use and generally speaking conceptive achievement.

C. Rearing and Regenerative Reactions
The timing and outcome of rearing seasons are basic marks of natural wellbeing for bird populaces. Changes in temperature, precipitation examples, and food accessibility impact reproducing ways of behaving, egg-laying, and chick-raising exercises. Changes in these examples might have flowing consequences for populace elements.

Perceptions of modified rearing phenology, remembering changes for the planning of egg-laying and fledging, have been connected to environmental change. Hotter temperatures can prompt prior springs, influencing the accessibility of bugs essential for taking care of little birds. Changes in rearing achievement, for example, home disappointment rates or chick endurance, give experiences into the effects of natural stressors on regenerative results.

III. Physiological Reactions
A. Hormonal Changes
Birds show physiological reactions to natural changes, with hormonal movements assuming a focal part in variation. Chemicals manage different parts of avian life cycles, including movement, propagation, and shedding. Changes in chemical levels can be demonstrative of pressure, modified regenerative techniques, or changes in energy allotment.

For example, openness to contaminations, like endocrine-upsetting synthetics, can slow down hormonal guideline in birds. Studies have demonstrated the way that openness to pesticides and modern poisons can upset regenerative chemicals, influencing fruitfulness and the suitability of bird populaces. Checking hormonal levels in birds gives bits of knowledge into the possible effects of natural pollutants.

B. Plumage and Hue Changes
The hue and state of bird plumage are affected by ecological factors and can act as marks of by and large wellbeing. Birds might show changes in feather tinge, quality, or examples in light of varieties in diet, openness to poisons, or climatic circumstances. For instance, studies have archived changes in the shading of quills in light of urbanization. Birds living in metropolitan conditions might encounter expanded openness to contaminations, prompting changes in feather shades. Checking plumage condition furnishes scientists with a painless strategy to evaluate the effect of ecological stressors on avian populaces.

C. Safe Framework Reactions
The safe arrangement of birds is intently attached to ecological circumstances, and changes in resistant reactions can demonstrate openness to microbes, contaminations, or different stressors. Checking invulnerable framework boundaries, for example, immunizer creation and white platelet counts, gives bits of knowledge into the strength of bird populaces.

For example, studies have researched the effect of environment corruption on the insusceptible capability of birds. Loss of regular environments, discontinuity, and openness to contaminations can think twice about resistant reactions of birds, making them more vulnerable to sicknesses. Evaluating safe framework wellbeing is significant for grasping the general flexibility of bird populaces despite natural changes.

IV. Environmental Reactions
A. Environment Movements
Changes in land use, deforestation, and urbanization impact bird territories, prompting shifts in conveyance and overflow.

Birds are exceptionally reliant upon explicit vegetation types, settling locales, and food sources, making them touchy signs of environment modifications.

Noticing changes in the circulation of bird species gives significant data about the effect of land-use changes. For instance, woodland discontinuity might prompt the segregation of bird populaces, influencing their capacity to track down reasonable mates and food assets. Observing these territory shifts is urgent for surveying the drawn out practicality of bird species in changed scenes.

B. Local area Elements

Bird people group, made out of different species connecting inside a biological system, answer ecological changes all in all. Modifications in local area structure, species lavishness, or creation can show shifts in biological system wellbeing and working.

For example, studies have exhibited the effect of obtrusive species on local bird networks. The presentation of non-local hunters or contenders can prompt decreases in local bird populaces. Checking changes in local area elements assists specialists with grasping the perplexing connections among species and the outcomes of natural aggravations.

C. Marker Species for Preservation Arranging

Certain bird species are assigned as marker species because of their aversion to explicit natural circumstances. These species can give early alerts of environment debasement or act as central focuses for protection arranging.

For instance, the presence of specific bird species might demonstrate the wellbeing of wetland environments. Waterfowl, swimming birds, and swamp staying species are many times thought about marks of wetland quality. Observing the overflow and variety of these pointer species illuminates preservation systems for wetland natural surroundings.

V. Contextual analyses of Aversion to Ecological Changes
A. Icy Settling Shorebirds

Icy settling shorebirds, for example, the Red Bunch and the Pectoral Sandpiper, feature aversion to environmental change. Hotter temperatures in the Cold lead to prior snowmelt, impacting the planning of bug hatches. These shorebirds, subject to bugs for food during rearing, may confront difficulties in synchronizing their settling exercises with top bug accessibility.

Studies have shown that changes in the planning of Icy settling shorebird relocation and propagation are happening, featuring the impact of environmental change on these species. Understanding these examples is vital for anticipating the future suitability of Icy biological systems and the bird species that depend on them.

B. Field Birds in Agrarian Scenes

Field birds, including the Bobolink and the Eastern Meadowlark, are delicate to changes in rural scenes. Heightening of agribusiness, changes in crop types, and expanded pesticide use influence the accessibility of appropriate settling and searching living spaces for these species.

Perceptions of declining populaces of prairie birds because of rural changes highlight the weakness of these species. Preservation endeavors zeroing in on keeping up with and reestablishing field living spaces are fundamental for saving the variety and wealth of meadow bird populaces.

VI. Protection Suggestions and The executives Procedures
A. Territory Protection and Reclamation

Saving and reestablishing normal territories are essential systems for relieving the effect of natural changes on birds. Preservation endeavors ought to zero in on keeping up with biodiversity-rich regions, safeguarding basic natural surroundings, and reestablishing corrupted environments.

For instance, wetland reclamation projects benefit waterbird populaces by giving fundamental rearing and taking care of grounds. Safeguarding these territories guarantees the endurance of marker species and keeps up with the general strength of wetland biological systems.

B. Environmental Change Moderation and Variation

Tending to environmental change is vital for the drawn out preservation of birds and their territories. Moderation procedures, like decreasing ozone harming substance outflows, are fundamental for forestalling further environment related disturbances. Also, variation procedures that emphasis on helping birds in acclimating to evolving conditions, for example, adjusted relocation courses or reproducing timing, are pivotal. Preservation arranging ought to consolidate environment brilliant methodologies to guarantee the flexibility of bird populaces. Safeguarded regions might should be decisively situated to represent likely changes in bird appropriations because of environmental change.

C. Economical Land Use Practices

Advancing maintainable land use rehearses is fundamental for limiting environment misfortune and discontinuity. Empowering practices, for example, agroforestry, maintainable horticulture, and dependable metropolitan arranging can assist with making scenes that help sound bird populaces.

For instance, agroforestry frameworks that coordinate trees with rural harvests give environment variety to birds. These frameworks upgrade by and large biodiversity and add to the protection of bird species adjusted to both forested and open conditions.

D. Contamination Control and Checking

Endeavors to control contamination, whether from pesticides, modern pollutants, or plastic waste, are imperative for safeguarding bird populaces. Carrying out and implementing guidelines that limit the utilization of hurtful synthetic compounds and contaminations add to the general soundness of biological systems.

Observing projects that track contamination levels in bird tissues, like plumes or blood, give significant information to evaluating the viability of contamination control measures. Recognizing contamination areas of interest and executing designated mediations assist with moderating the effect of toxins on bird wellbeing.

E. Resident Science and Public Commitment

Drawing in the general population in bird checking through resident science drives encourages a feeling of ecological stewardship. Resident researchers contribute important information on bird sightings, ways of behaving, and populace patterns, increasing the endeavors of expert scientists.

Instructive projects and effort endeavors that feature the significance of birds as marks of natural wellbeing bring issues to light and support preservation activity. Public help is vital for executing compelling strategies and protection measures.

VII. Difficulties and Future Bearings
A. Worldwide Scale Difficulties

Addressing the responsiveness of birds to ecological really impacts requires a worldwide viewpoint. Many bird species embrace broad relocations, crossing worldwide limits. Cooperative endeavors among nations are fundamental for the protection of transient species and the conservation of basic natural surroundings along their movement courses.

Worldwide difficulties, for example, environmental change and living space misfortune, require facilitated activities on a global scale. Peaceful accords, for example, the Show on Transitory Species and the Ramsar Show on Wetlands, assume urgent parts in working with transboundary protection endeavors.

B. Coordinating Numerous Stressors

Birds frequently face numerous stressors at the same time, including environment misfortune, contamination, environmental change, and intrusive species. Understanding the intuitive impacts of these stressors is an intricate test. Incorporated approaches that consider the total effects on bird populaces are fundamental for viable preservation arranging.

For example, a comprehensive comprehension of how environmental change collaborates with living space corruption and contamination is fundamental for anticipating the strength of bird species. Research that examines these synergistic impacts adds to more educated and nuanced preservation methodologies.

C. Arising Innovations and Exploration Strategies

Progressions in innovation, like satellite following, remote detecting, and sub-atomic apparatuses, offer new roads for concentrating on bird aversion to ecological changes. Satellite following, for instance, gives bits of knowledge into bird relocation courses and natural surroundings use on a worldwide scale. These innovations upgrade the accuracy and extent of exploration, permitting researchers to screen bird populaces and ways of behaving with remarkable detail.

Consolidating hereditary instruments, for example, DNA investigation, assists scientists with understanding the populace construction, availability, and flexibility of bird species. Coordinating these arising innovations into existing observing and research programs improves our capacity to survey the mind boggling associations among birds and their surroundings.

D. Long haul Checking and Versatile Administration

Long haul observing projects are critical for following patterns in bird populaces and distinguishing changes over the long haul. The unique idea of natural circumstances requires versatile administration methodologies that can answer advancing difficulties. Preservation endeavors ought to be adaptable, integrating new data and changing procedures in view of continuous observing and research.

For instance, a drawn out observing system following the rearing progress of a bird animal groups can give bits of knowledge into what changing ecological circumstances mean for regenerative results. Versatile administration procedures might include changing territory rebuilding needs or altering protection mediations in light of the advancing necessities of bird populaces.

3.2   Monitoring Bird Populations for Ecosystem Health

Observing bird populaces is a basic part of understanding and keeping up with biological system wellbeing. Birds, as different and far reaching species, assume vital parts in environmental cycles like fertilization, seed dispersal, and bug control. They likewise act as marks of more extensive natural circumstances, reflecting changes in living space quality, environment, and the presence of poisons. This extensive investigation digs into the significance of observing bird populaces for biological system wellbeing, talking about techniques, key markers, and the more extensive ramifications for preservation and practical environment the executives.

II. Significance of Birds in Environments
A. Natural Jobs
Birds contribute fundamentally to the working of environments through different biological jobs. One of their essential capabilities is fertilization, a critical cycle for the propagation of blossoming plants. Many bird species, like hummingbirds and sunbirds, are skilled pollinators, working with the development of leafy foods.
Birds likewise assume a key part in seed dispersal. As they scrounge for food, birds eat products of the soil seeds across scenes. This cycle helps in the recovery of plant populaces and adds to the biodiversity and flexibility of biological systems.
Insectivorous birds go about as normal bug regulators by consuming huge amounts of bugs. This predation directs bug populaces, forestalling episodes that could adversely affect crops or other plant species. The presence of birds hence adds to an equilibrium in bug populaces and supports generally speaking environment wellbeing.

B. Marker Species
Birds are delicate to natural changes and act as important signs of environment wellbeing. Their reactions to changes in territory quality, contamination levels, and environment conditions give early alerts of aggravations that might influence more extensive biological cycles. Observing bird populaces permits researchers and traditionalists to follow these reactions and survey the general strength of biological systems.
For instance, decreases in specific bird species might demonstrate territory corruption, loss of food assets, or the presence of poisons. Then again, the fruitful preservation of specific bird populaces might mean powerful territory the executives and supportable environment rehearses.

III. Techniques for Observing Bird Populaces
A. Bird Studies and Registration Procedures
Bird studies and censuses are central techniques for checking bird populaces. These exercises include efficiently counting and recording bird species and their overflows inside a particular region. Different study procedures, for example, point counts, cut across reviews, and fog netting, furnish analysts with significant information on bird circulation and overflow.
Point counts include fixed onlookers recording all birds seen or heard inside an assigned sweep during a predefined time. Cut across studies include strolling along foreordained ways and recording bird sightings. Fog netting is a procedure where fine nets are utilized to catch birds for distinguishing proof, estimation, and checking before discharge. These techniques offer bits of knowledge into populace size, species extravagance, and changes in appropriation over the long run.

B. Resident Science Drives

Connecting with general society in bird observing through resident science drives has become progressively well known. Undertakings like eBird, BirdTrack, and the Christmas Bird include resident researchers in recording bird perceptions. These commitments altogether extend the spatial and transient inclusion of bird observing endeavors.

Resident science drives give enormous datasets to scientists as well as cultivate public commitment to protection. Members in these projects contribute important data about bird conveyances, transitory examples, and changes in overflow, upgrading how we might interpret bird populaces at a worldwide scale.

C. Bird Banding and Following

Bird banding includes connecting particularly numbered groups to a bird's leg for distinguishing proof. This strategy permits specialists to follow individual birds over the long haul, assemble data on relocation designs, reproducing achievement, and endurance rates. Propels in innovation have prompted the improvement of satellite GPS beacons and geolocators, giving constant information on bird developments and ways of behaving.

Following individual birds assists specialists with understanding their developments, relocation courses, and the particular natural surroundings they use. This data is urgent for distinguishing key regions for protection and overseeing biological systems to help the necessities of transient species.

D. Bioacoustics Observing

Bioacoustics, the investigation of creature sounds, is an inexorably significant apparatus for observing bird populaces. Propels in innovation, for example, independent recording units and AI calculations, permit scientists to dissect and decipher bird vocalizations. Bioacoustic checking is especially helpful in regions with thick vegetation or testing landscape where visual overviews might be less successful.

Recording and dissecting bird calls give data about species presence, action examples, and changes in vocal way of behaving. This technique isn't just painless yet additionally considers consistent checking, giving important bits of knowledge into bird populaces overstretched periods.

IV. Key Pointers in Bird Populace Checking
A. Species Lavishness and Variety

Species lavishness and variety are crucial signs of biological system wellbeing. Observing the quantity of bird species in a given region gives bits of knowledge into the general biodiversity and environmental trustworthiness of a biological system.

Decreases in species wealth might demonstrate natural surroundings corruption, while an expansion in variety might propose viable preservation measures.

Changes in the piece of bird networks additionally offer important data. For instance, an expansion within the sight of obtrusive species might flag disturbances in biological system balance, while decreases in local species might show territory misfortune or other ecological stressors.

B. Populace Overflow and Patterns

Checking the wealth of bird populaces and following populace patterns after some time are basic for evaluating the strength of environments. Populace declines might be demonstrative of environment misfortune, contamination, or different dangers. On the other hand, expansions in populace overflow might recommend effective preservation endeavors or changes in land utilize that benefit specific species.

Long haul populace pattern information assist specialists with recognizing examples and expected dangers, taking into account designated preservation mediations. Understanding whether populaces are steady, expanding, or declining gives a premise to informed dynamic in environment the board.

C. Rearing Achievement and Conceptive Boundaries

Evaluating rearing achievement and conceptive boundaries is fundamental for grasping the regenerative strength of bird populaces. Checking elements like home achievement, juvenile endurance, and regenerative result gives experiences into the effect of ecological circumstances on reproducing results.

Changes in rearing achievement might be connected to adjustments in environment quality, food accessibility, or the presence of contaminations. For instance, decreases in home achievement might demonstrate the effect of pesticide openness or changes in food accessibility, underscoring the requirement for designated protection measures.

D. Transitory Examples

Observing the transient examples of birds is pivotal for understanding their life cycles and recognizing key natural surroundings along relocation courses. Many bird species depend on unambiguous visit locales for rest and refueling during movement. These regions are basic for their endurance and regenerative achievement.

Changes in transient examples, like changes in timing or courses, might be characteristic of environmental change or adjustments in living space quality. Checking transitory examples distinguishes significant visit destinations, empowering the execution of preservation measures to safeguard these essential regions.

E. Wellbeing and Illness Observation

Observing the soundness of bird populaces includes evaluating variables like sickness pervasiveness, physiological boundaries, and openness to impurities. Observation for avian infections, like avian flu or West Nile infection, is fundamental for both bird and general wellbeing.

Also, evaluating the physiological soundness of birds, including body condition, invulnerable capability, and hormonal profiles, gives bits of knowledge into their capacity to adapt to ecological stressors. Checking for openness to poisons, for example, weighty metals or pesticides, distinguishes possible dangers to bird populaces and environments.

V. Suggestions for Preservation and Biological system The executives

A. Recognizing Dangers and Focusing on Preservation Activities

Observing bird populaces permits specialists to recognize dangers to biological systems and focus on preservation activities. For instance, decreases in bird species related with explicit environments might flag the requirement for natural surroundings rebuilding or assurance. Understanding the elements adding to populace declines empowers traditionalists to carry out designated intercessions.

Dangers, for example, territory misfortune, environmental change, contamination, and intrusive species can be tended to through essential protection arranging. By zeroing in on key pointers from bird observing endeavors, protection activities can be customized to address the particular necessities of environments and the species that possess them.

B. Evaluating the Adequacy of Protection Measures

Observing bird populaces gives a way to survey the viability of preservation estimates after some time. For example, in the event that natural surroundings rebuilding endeavors are executed to help a particular bird animal varieties, observing populace patterns when reclamation gives experiences into the outcome of the mediation. Preservation examples of overcoming adversity, like the recuperation of imperiled species, frequently include long haul checking endeavors. Surveying populace reactions to preservation activities refines systems and adjust the executives approaches in light of continuous criticism from observed populaces.

C. Biological system Administrations and Human Prosperity

Birds add to biological system benefits that benefit human prosperity. For instance, insectivorous birds give normal nuisance control, diminishing the requirement for synthetic pesticides in horticulture. Pollinator birds add to the creation of products of the soil, supporting food security.

Checking bird populaces evaluates the biological system administrations given by birds and features the interconnectedness between solid environments and human prosperity. Perceiving the worth of birds in environment working supports the significance of their protection for feasible and strong scenes.

D. Environmental Change Transformation Methodologies

As environmental change keeps on influencing biological systems, observing bird populaces becomes critical for adjusting preservation procedures. Changes in the dissemination and conduct of bird species are in many cases early signs of environment prompted shifts in living space appropriateness.

Understanding how bird populaces answer environmental change educates the improvement regarding transformation methodologies. For instance, distinguishing regions where certain species are growing their reaches focuses on preservation endeavors in locales that might turn out to be progressively significant for biodiversity under changing climatic circumstances.

VI. Difficulties and Future Bearings

A. Information Quality and Normalization

One test in checking bird populaces is guaranteeing the quality and normalization of information. Different checking strategies, eyewitness predispositions, and varieties in information assortment conventions can present irregularities. Addressing these difficulties requires continuous endeavors to normalize checking conventions, train onlookers, and carry out quality control measures.

Headways in innovation, for example, computerized recording gadgets and AI calculations, offer chances to improve information quality and smooth out examination. Normalizing information assortment techniques guarantees the likeness of results across various areas and time spans.

B. Tending to Spatial and Transient Inconstancy

Bird populaces show spatial and worldly inconstancy, making it trying to catch thorough depictions of their status. Movement, occasional changes, and varieties in reproducing conduct add to this fluctuation. Observing endeavors need to represent these elements to give exact evaluations of populace status.

Long haul checking programs that length numerous seasons and years assist with tending to fleeting changeability. Moreover, consolidating information from different locales and living spaces helps catch the spatial variety of bird populaces. Understanding how birds answer changes across various scenes adds to a more complete comprehension of their biology.

C. Incorporating Numerous Stressors

Birds frequently face various stressors all the while, including territory misfortune, contamination, environmental change, and intrusive species. Incorporating information on these numerous stressors is fundamental for a comprehensive comprehension of the difficulties bird populaces experience.

Future examination ought to zero in on explaining the collaborations between various stressors and their aggregate impacts on bird populaces. This coordinated methodology will give a more nuanced comprehension of the intricacies of biological system elements and backing the improvement of designated preservation techniques.

D. Public Commitment and Instruction

Advancing public commitment to bird checking and protection is fundamental for the progress of observing projects. While resident science drives have taken critical steps, continuous endeavors to teach general society about the significance of birds and their job in environments are pivotal.

Training and effort programs that feature the worth of birds in keeping up with biological system wellbeing foster a feeling of ecological stewardship. Drawing in networks in bird checking exercises contributes important information as well as reinforces the association among individuals and their neighborhood surroundings.

E. Versatile Administration and Strength

Versatile administration methodologies are important to address the powerful idea of biological systems and the vulnerabilities related with ecological changes. Checking projects ought to be planned with adaptability, considering versatile reactions to arising dangers or unforeseen results.

Understanding the versatility of bird populaces to natural changes illuminates versatile administration draws near. Building strength in biological systems includes keeping up with natural surroundings network, safeguarding key environmental cycles, and tending to dangers proactively. Versatile administration guarantees that preservation procedures stay powerful notwithstanding advancing difficulties.

Chapter 4
Threats to Avian Biodiversity

Avian biodiversity, the assortment of bird species in a specific territory or on Earth overall, is a basic part of worldwide biodiversity. Birds assume significant parts in biological systems, adding to processes like fertilization, seed dispersal, bug control, and supplement cycling. Furthermore, they are fundamental signs of natural wellbeing, reflecting changes in biological systems and environment. Nonetheless, avian biodiversity faces a horde of dangers, both regular and anthropogenic, that imperil the endurance of numerous species. In this extensive investigation, we will dig into the different elements that posture dangers to avian biodiversity, going from living space misfortune and environmental change to contamination and obtrusive species.

Natural surroundings Misfortune and Discontinuity
One of the main dangers to avian biodiversity is natural surroundings misfortune and discontinuity. Human exercises, like deforestation, urbanization, and horticultural development, have prompted the annihilation of normal living spaces that birds depend on for rearing, taking care of, and settling. As woods are cleared for lumber, agribusiness, or foundation advancement, many bird species lose their homes and face difficulties in tracking down appropriate other options.
Fracture further compounds the issue, as outstanding territories become separated from one another. This detachment can obstruct the development of bird populaces, making it hard for them to track down mates, food, and appropriate rearing locales. Subsequently, the hereditary variety of populaces can diminish, making them more vulnerable to sicknesses and natural changes.

Environmental Change
Environmental change is a worldwide peculiarity that has expansive ramifications for avian biodiversity. Changes in temperature, precipitation designs, and the recurrence and force of outrageous climate occasions can affect the appropriation and conduct of bird species. Many birds depend on unambiguous climatic circumstances for reproducing, relocation, and taking care of, and adjustments in these circumstances can upset their life cycles.
Climbing temperatures can likewise prompt changes in the conveyance of plant and bug species, influencing the accessibility of nourishment for birds. A few animal types might battle to adjust to these changes, prompting decreases in populace size or even nearby terminations. Moreover, ocean level ascent represents a danger to beach front bird natural surroundings, driving species to move inland or face territory misfortune.

Contamination

Different types of contamination present huge dangers to avian biodiversity. Water contamination, brought about by modern spillover, agrarian pesticides, and oil slicks, can debase amphibian biological systems and influence water-subordinate bird species. Likewise, air contamination, coming about because of modern outflows and vehicle exhaust, can unfavorably affect birds by corrupting air quality and influencing respiratory frameworks.

Synthetic contaminations, like pesticides and herbicides, can enter the pecking order, influencing both insectivorous and granivorous birds. These synthetics might prompt decreases in bug populaces, diminishing the food accessible for bug eating birds, or they can straightforwardly harm birds that polish off defiled food or water.

Obtrusive Species

The acquaintance of non-local species with new conditions can have serious ramifications for local bird populaces. Intrusive species, whether plants, creatures, or microorganisms, can outcompete local species for assets, present new sicknesses, and upset laid out biological connections.

For instance, obtrusive hunters like rodents, felines, and snakes have been answerable for the downfall or annihilation of numerous island bird species that advanced without such hunters. These presented species frequently exploit the absence of normal guards in island biological systems, going after birds and their eggs without powerful regular hunters to hold their populaces within proper limits.

Overexploitation and Hunting

By and large, overexploitation through hunting and catching has prompted the downfall of various bird species. While preservation endeavors and guidelines have relieved a portion of these dangers, unlawful hunting and the exchange of birds and their eggs keep on presenting gambles, especially in districts with powerless requirement of untamed life security regulations.

Certain species, valued for their plumage, melody, or as intriguing pets, are especially defenseless. The interest for these birds in the pet exchange has prompted the consumption of populaces nature. Furthermore, conventional hunting rehearses for food and social reasons can likewise affect bird populaces, particularly in regions with high human reliance on normal assets.

Illness

Illness flare-ups, whether regular or presented, can devastatingly affect avian biodiversity.

Avian flu, for instance, has caused critical mortality in wild bird populaces and has raised worries about its possible transmission to homegrown poultry and people. Different infections, like West Nile infection and avian intestinal sickness, can likewise influence bird populaces.

Territory corruption and environmental change can impact the predominance and circulation of infections, influencing the wellbeing and endurance of bird species. Birds with restricted hereditary opposition or those generally pushed by other ecological variables might be more defenseless to illness flare-ups, prompting populace declines.

Worldwide Exchange and Transportation

Globalization has worked with the development of merchandise and individuals across borders, coincidentally supporting the spread of obtrusive species, sicknesses, and contaminations. The worldwide exchange natural life, including birds, adds to the acquaintance of non-local species with new areas. Birds caught for the pet exchange might convey illnesses or parasites that can be acquainted with new regions when they are sold and shipped.

In addition, the development of transportation organizations, including delivery and air travel, can speed up the spread of illnesses among bird populaces. Contaminated birds might convey microbes to new locales during relocation, expanding the gamble of infection transmission between populaces.

Changes in Land Use

Human exercises that adjust land use, like horticulture, logging, and framework advancement, can significantly affect avian biodiversity. Horticultural escalation, for instance, may prompt the change of different normal living spaces into monoculture scenes, restricting the accessibility of food and appropriate settling locales for the overwhelming majority bird species.

Urbanization likewise changes regular scenes into counterfeit conditions, with structures, streets, and different designs supplanting normal natural surroundings. While some bird species might adjust to metropolitan conditions, numerous others can't flourish in such changed scenes, prompting decreases in their populaces.

4.1   Habitat Loss and Fragmentation

Environment misfortune and discontinuity are two interconnected processes that present critical dangers to avian biodiversity. As human exercises keep on adjusting scenes for different purposes, normal environments urgent for the endurance of various bird species are vanishing at a disturbing rate. Understanding the elements of natural surroundings misfortune and discontinuity is fundamental for contriving viable protection procedures to relieve their effect on avian populaces.

1. Territory Misfortune
Definition and Causes:
Natural surroundings misfortune alludes to the through and through obliteration or huge
decrease of a specific living space, delivering it unsatisfactory for the species that rely
upon it. Human exercises are the essential drivers of environment misfortune, and these
incorporate deforestation, urbanization, agribusiness, and foundation advancement. As
the worldwide populace develops and economies grow, the interest for land heightens,
prompting the transformation of normal environments into regions for development,
settlement, or industry.

Influence on Avian Biodiversity:
The repercussions of territory misfortune on avian biodiversity are significant. Birds
depend on unambiguous natural surroundings for reproducing, settling, taking care of,
and movement. At the point when these natural surroundings are annihilated or
changed, bird populaces face quick difficulties. Species adjusted to specific biological
systems might battle to find appropriate other options, prompting decreases in populace
size and, in outrageous cases, nearby eradications. Besides, territory misfortune
frequently brings about the discontinuity of once persistent scenes, intensifying the
difficulties for avian species.

2. Discontinuity
Definition and Instruments:
Discontinuity happens when huge, nonstop territories are partitioned into more modest,
segregated patches. This cycle disturbs the spatial network of biological systems and
can happen as an immediate outcome of environment misfortune or through the
production of obstructions like streets, metropolitan regions, or horticultural fields.
Divided natural surroundings become isolated by regions that are cold or unacceptable
for the species that once navigated the scene uninhibitedly.

Ramifications for Birds:
Discontinuity represents various difficulties for avian species. The detachment of living
space, right off the bat, patches can block the development of bird populaces. Birds
frequently need to move between reproducing, taking care of, and wintering grounds,
and divided scenes make these excursions more troublesome. The seclusion can
prompt diminished hereditary variety inside populaces, making them more vulnerable to
infections and less versatile to natural changes.
Furthermore, the edges of divided living spaces, known as ecotones, may encounter
modified microclimates and expanded openness to predation. This can make a "edge
impact," affecting the overflow and dissemination of bird species.

A few animal groups adjusted to the inside of enormous, nonstop natural surroundings might stay away from or battle to flourish in the changed circumstances at the edges.

Interconnected Difficulties
Living space misfortune and discontinuity are not disconnected dangers but rather are much of the time interweaved processes. As territories contract, they become more vulnerable to fracture, compounding the difficulties looked by avian populaces. For example, a divided scene might comprise of segregated patches of debased territory, further decreasing the general quality and usefulness of the environment. Furthermore, living space misfortune can be a forerunner to fracture. As enormous regions are changed over for farming or metropolitan turn of events, the leftover regular territories might become confined, encompassed by scopes of inadmissible land. This segregation can prompt the fracture of once-associated environments, restricting the capacity of birds to move between various pieces of their natural surroundings.

Protection Suggestions
Relieving the effect of natural surroundings misfortune and fracture requires extensive preservation methodologies that address the two cycles all the while. The accompanying methodologies are pivotal:

Natural surroundings Safeguarding: Focus on the insurance and preservation of basic living spaces for avian biodiversity. This incorporates distinguishing and shielding regions that act as favorable places, movement courses, and wintering living spaces.

Hall Creation: Lay out natural life passages to interface divided territories. These passageways give roads to the development of bird populaces, working with quality stream and keeping up with environmental cycles. Halls can be normal highlights or human-made structures intended to permit safe section for natural life.

Maintainable Land Use Practices: Advance economical land the board practices to offset human improvement with the protection of regular natural surroundings. This incorporates taking on agroforestry, advancing green metropolitan preparation, and executing dependable logging rehearses.

Reclamation Endeavors: Attempt natural surroundings rebuilding tasks to restore debased regions and reconnect divided scenes. This can include establishing local vegetation, eliminating hindrances, and upgrading the general nature of environments.

Local area Commitment: Include neighborhood networks in preservation endeavors, as they frequently assume a critical part in the practical utilization of normal assets.

Local area drove drives can add to living space safeguarding and lessen the tensions driving natural surroundings misfortune.

4.2   Climate Change and Its Impact on Bird Habitats

Environmental change, driven generally by human exercises like the consuming of petroleum products and deforestation, is quite possibly of the most squeezing challenge confronting our planet. The results of a warming environment reach out across biological systems, influencing species and territories in different ways. Birds, being profoundly delicate to ecological changes, face huge difficulties as their living spaces go through modifications in temperature, precipitation examples, and generally environment conditions. In this exhaustive investigation, we will dig into the complexities of environmental change and its significant effect on bird territories, looking at how shifts in environment factors impact avian biodiversity, appropriation, and conduct.

1. Temperature Changes and Reproducing Achievement
Warming Environments and Settling Phenology:

Climbing worldwide temperatures have suggestions for the planning of key occasions in bird life cycles, like reproducing and settling. Changes in temperature impact the phenology of plants and the accessibility of bug prey, which, thusly, influence the planning of bird reproducing seasons. Many bird species time their regenerative endeavors to match with the pinnacle accessibility of food assets for their chicks.
As temperatures climb, the planning of spring occasions, like the rise of bugs and the blossoming of plants, can move. In the event that birds don't change their rearing seasons likewise, there might be a confuse between the bring forth of chicks and the wealth of fundamental food sources. This confound can inconveniently affect the endurance and conceptive outcome of bird populaces.

Influence on Transient Species:

For transient bird species, environmental change presents novel difficulties. Birds that embrace significant distance relocations depend on ecological prompts, like temperature and day length, to time their excursions. Changes in environment can upset these signals, prompting confuses between the planning of relocation and the accessibility of reasonable rearing and taking care of grounds.
Moreover, the expanded recurrence and force of outrageous climate occasions, like tempests and heatwaves, can present direct dangers to transient birds during their excursions. For instance, extreme climate occasions can influence the accessibility of visit destinations, where birds rest and refuel during relocation, possibly affecting their general wellness and capacity to effectively finish their movements.

2. Adjusted Conveyance Examples
Changes in Reach and Natural surroundings Appropriateness:

Environmental change is causing shifts in the geological scopes of many bird species as they answer changes in temperature and precipitation. Species that were once limited to explicit scopes or rises might move poleward or to higher heights looking for reasonable environments.

While certain species might find recently reasonable territories because of these movements, others might confront difficulties assuming their ongoing natural surroundings become inadmissible. This can prompt changes in local area structure, with likely effects on aggressive communications, hunter prey connections, and generally biological system elements.

Rugged Territories and Elevational Changes:

Rugged locales are especially helpless against the effects of environmental change, as temperature changes at higher heights can be more articulated than at lower rises. Species adjusted to explicit temperature reaches might be compelled to move upslope to keep up with appropriate circumstances.

The results of elevational changes are complicated. As birds move to higher rises, they might experience new contenders and hunters, possibly prompting shifts in local area structure. Moreover, species that are now at the most noteworthy rises might confront the deficiency of reasonable territory as they arrive at the mountain's highest point, with restricted choices for additional upslope development.

3. Territory Misfortune and Discontinuity
Far and wide Living space Changes:

Environmental change adds to natural surroundings misfortune and corruption, intensifying the difficulties looked by birds. Expanded temperatures, modified precipitation examples, and outrageous climate occasions can prompt the debasement of biological systems, influencing the accessibility of food, water, and reasonable settling destinations.

Ocean level ascent, driven by the dissolving of polar ice and icy masses, represents a danger to seaside territories involved by many bird species for rearing and scrounging. As ocean levels rise, settling locales might be immersed, and seaside environments might go through critical changes, affecting the birds that rely upon them.

Influence on Icy and Antarctic Living spaces:

Polar locales are encountering the absolute most fast changes because of environment warming.

In the Icy, defrosting permafrost and diminished ocean ice inclusion are changing the environments involved by various bird species for rearing and rummaging. Species like the Icy Tern, Frigid Owl, and different waterfowl are confronting difficulties as their customary favorable places go through changes in temperature and ice cover.

In the Antarctic, warming temperatures are influencing the dispersion and wealth of krill, a basic food hotspot for some seabirds. Changes in ocean ice elements additionally influence the accessibility of settling destinations for species like penguins and seabirds, further featuring the broad results of environmental change on bird living spaces.

4. Maritime Changes and Seabirds
Sea Warming and Fermentation:
The world's seas assume an essential part in supporting marine life, including a different exhibit of seabird species. Be that as it may, environmental change is causing huge changes in sea conditions, with climbing temperatures and sea fermentation being two key results.

Warming sea temperatures influence the circulation and overflow of prey species, affecting the scavenging progress of seabirds. Changes in ocean surface temperatures can likewise impact sea flows, which, thus, influence the accessibility of supplements and the dissemination of marine life.

Sea fermentation, coming about because of the assimilation of overabundance carbon dioxide via seawater, represents extra difficulties for seabirds. The fermentation of seas can influence the accessibility of calcium carbonate, a basic part for the development of shells and skeletons of marine creatures that comprise the eating routine of numerous seabirds.

Changes in Prey Accessibility:
Seabirds are profoundly reliant upon the accessibility of fish and other marine creatures for their endurance. Environment actuated changes in sea temperatures can prompt changes in the circulation and wealth of these prey species. This, thus, influences the rummaging progress of seabirds, as they might have to travel longer distances or adjust to new taking care of grounds.

For species, for example, gooney birds and petrels, which have enormous rummaging ranges, changes in prey accessibility can have flowing consequences for their regenerative achievement. Decreased admittance to food during the reproducing season can bring about lower chick endurance rates and populace declines.

5. Outrageous Climate Occasions
Heightening of Outrageous Occasions:
Environmental change is related with an expanded recurrence and power of outrageous climate occasions, including typhoons, dry seasons, heatwaves, and storms.

These occasions can by implication affect bird territories, impacting food accessibility, home security, and in general biological system wellbeing.

Storm Floods and Beach front Disintegration:
Seaside natural surroundings, fundamental for the vast majority bird species during rearing and movement, are especially defenseless against the effects of outrageous climate occasions. Storm floods, driven by typhoons or hurricanes, can immerse settling destinations, obliterate vegetation, and lead to the deficiency of urgent environments. Beach front disintegration, exacerbated via ocean level ascent and expanded storm recurrence, can additionally decrease the accessibility of appropriate settling destinations for shorebirds and seabirds. Species that home on sea shores, hills, or bluffs might confront expanded dangers of home disappointment because of the destabilization of these environments.

6. Protection Systems and Variation
Territory The executives and Reclamation:
Protection systems to address the effects of environmental change on bird territories frequently include natural surroundings the board and rebuilding endeavors. This incorporates distinguishing and safeguarding basic living spaces, reestablishing debased regions, and making support zones to consider the normal development of species because of evolving environments.
For instance, safeguarding mangrove backwoods and waterfront wetlands can relieve the effects of ocean level ascent on shorebird environments. Also, reforestation projects in bumpy areas can furnish bird species with upslope relocation pathways, permitting them to follow appropriate environments.

Environment Strong Passage Plan:
Establishing environment versatile passages is one more urgent part of protection arranging. These hallways work with the development of species across scenes, permitting them to adjust to changing climatic circumstances. Passageways can interface divided living spaces, empowering birds to move, scatter, and look for appropriate conditions on a case by case basis.
Planning passageways that record for possible future changes in temperature and precipitation designs is fundamental. Safeguarded regions and untamed life saves associated by all around planned passageways can improve the general versatility of biological systems and advance hereditary variety inside bird populaces.

Local area Commitment and Resident Science:
Despite environmental change, local area commitment and resident science drives assume urgent parts in checking bird populaces and living spaces.

Nearby people group frequently have important information about changes in bird conduct, movement designs, and the accessibility of assets.

Empowering resident researchers to take part in bird observing projects can furnish scientists with important information that add to how we might interpret what environmental change is meaning for bird territories. This commitment encourages a feeling of shared liability regarding natural stewardship and can illuminate versatile administration systems at nearby and territorial scales.

Strategy and Worldwide Joint effort:
Tending to the difficulties presented by environmental change requires composed endeavors at public and global levels. Policymakers assume a urgent part in carrying out guidelines and motivations that advance supportable practices, lessen ozone harming substance discharges, and safeguard basic natural surroundings. Worldwide joint effort is fundamental for the preservation of transitory bird species that cross numerous nations during their excursions. Arrangements like the Show on Transitory Species (CMS) and the Ramsar Show on Wetlands give systems to worldwide collaboration in the security of basic bird territories.

4.3   Pollution and Its Effects on Bird Populations

Contamination, emerging from different human exercises, represents a huge and inescapable danger to biological systems around the world. Birds, being exceptionally delicate to changes in their current circumstance, are significantly impacted by various types of contamination. This incorporates air and water contamination, as well as the presentation of compound toxins. In this investigation, we will dive into the effects of contamination on bird populaces, analyzing what it means for their wellbeing, reproducing achievement, and generally endurance.

1. Air Contamination:
a. Respiratory Issues:
Air contamination, basically determined by the burning of petroleum derivatives, modern emanations, and agrarian practices, can significantly affect bird populaces. Birds, with their profoundly productive respiratory frameworks, are especially powerless against airborne contaminations like particulate matter, nitrogen oxides, and sulfur dioxide. Openness to elevated degrees of air poisons can prompt respiratory issues in birds, influencing their capacity to inhale and, thusly, their general wellbeing. Species living in metropolitan conditions or close to modern regions might confront constant openness to poisons, affecting their drawn out prosperity.

b. Modified Conduct and Rummaging:
Air contamination can likewise impact bird conduct. Studies have shown that specific poisons, like ozone, can upset the compound organization of botanical fragrances utilized by birds to find blossoms and food. This can bring about modified searching examples as birds battle to find fundamental assets.
Moreover, commotion contamination related with metropolitan regions and transportation organizations can influence bird correspondence, obstructing mating calls and regional signs. These interruptions can have flowing impacts on reproducing achievement and populace elements.

2. Water Contamination:
a. Polluted Oceanic Biological systems:
Water contamination, brought about by modern releases, farming spillover, and inappropriate garbage removal, has extreme ramifications for bird species that depend on sea-going environments for taking care of and rearing. Amphibian birds, like waterfowl and swimming birds, are especially defenseless against the pollution of wetlands, waterways, and waterfront regions.
Contaminations like weighty metals, pesticides, and oil can amass in the tissues of oceanic creatures, entering the well established pecking order. Birds that feed on sullied prey might experience the ill effects of decreased conceptive achievement, formative irregularities, and compromised invulnerable frameworks.

b. Influence on Regenerative Achievement:
Water contamination can straightforwardly affect the regenerative outcome of birds. Many bird species lay their eggs in homes situated close to water bodies, and the nature of water in these territories is critical for the wellbeing and advancement of chicks. Impurities, for example, mercury and PCBs can prompt eggshell diminishing, influencing the reasonability of eggs and expanding the gamble of home disappointment.

3. Synthetic Poisons:
a. Pesticides and Herbicides:
The utilization of pesticides and herbicides in agribusiness has boundless ramifications for bird populaces. Birds that feed on bugs or seeds treated with these synthetic compounds might ingest destructive substances, prompting intense harming or persistent medical problems.
Pesticides, for example, neonicotinoids, can have sublethal impacts on birds, influencing their capacity to explore, track down food, and replicate. Moreover, the downfall of bug populaces because of pesticide use can influence insectivorous bird species that depend on bugs as an essential food source.

b. Bioaccumulation and Biomagnification:
Synthetic poisons can possibly collect and amplify through food networks, an interaction known as bioaccumulation and biomagnification. Birds at higher trophic levels, like raptors and dominant hunters, are especially powerless with the impacts of biomagnification. Impurities aggregate in their tissues at fixations a lot higher than those in their prey.
This biomagnification can prompt regenerative issues, impeded safe capability, and even populace declines. For instance, the pesticide DDT, albeit prohibited in numerous nations, keeps on affecting bird populaces through lingering tainting that continues in the climate.

4. Light Contamination:
a. Interruption of Circadian Rhythms:
Light contamination, brought about by the unreasonable or misled fake brightening of the night sky, can upset the normal ways of behaving of nighttime and transient birds. Many bird species depend on the normal patterns of light and haziness to control their circadian rhythms, including taking care of, mating, and relocation.
Fake lights can muddle birds, prompting impacts with structures, correspondence towers, and different designs. Nighttime travelers might become drawn to splendid lights, revolving around and depleting themselves in what is known as "deadly light fascination." These disturbances can bring about wounds, mortality, and obstruction with urgent life cycle occasions.

Preservation Techniques:
Tending to contamination and its consequences for bird populaces requires a complex methodology:

Administrative Measures: Execute and implement guidelines that limit emanations and releases of toxins very high and water. Stricter controls on modern cycles, horticultural practices, and garbage removal can relieve the effect of contamination on bird environments.

Environment Security: Shielding regular natural surroundings, including wetlands, waterfront regions, and metropolitan green spaces, is fundamental for keeping up with sound bird populaces. Safeguarded regions go about as shelters where birds can find appropriate living spaces liberated from the immediate effects of contamination.

Elective Agrarian Practices: Advance and boost reasonable and natural cultivating rehearses that lessen the dependence on synthetic pesticides and herbicides.

Coordinated bug the executives and agroecological approaches can relieve the adverse consequences of rural synthetic compounds on birds.

Public Mindfulness and Training: Bring issues to light about the effects of contamination on bird populaces through schooling and effort programs. Support capable garbage removal, diminished utilization of single-use plastics, and different practices that limit ecological contamination.

Checking and Exploration: Backing research drives and observing projects to survey the degree of contamination and its impacts on bird populaces. Long haul reads up give important information to grasping patterns, distinguishing arising dangers, and illuminating preservation techniques.

4.4   Invasive Species and Competition for Resources

The acquaintance of non-local species with new conditions, whether purposeful or unexpected, has turned into a worldwide peculiarity with extensive natural results. Intrusive species, frequently described by quick proliferation and productive asset usage, can outcompete and adversely influence local widely varied vegetation. Birds, being necessary parts of biological systems, are especially powerless with the impacts of intrusive species. In this investigation, we will dig into the natural ramifications of obtrusive species and the opposition for assets, zeroing in on how these collaborations shape bird populaces and their living spaces.

1. Meaning of Obtrusive Species:

Obtrusive species are non-local living beings that, when acquainted with another climate, lay out self-supporting populaces and spread quickly, frequently outcompeting local species for assets. Birds, as versatile creatures, can work with the unexpected spread of intrusive species by moving seeds or propagules across scenes. This accidental dispersal can prompt the foundation of obtrusive species in new regions, further fueling rivalry for assets.

2. Rivalry for Settling Destinations:
a. Home Site Rejection:

Obtrusive species can rival local birds for restricted settling destinations, a basic asset for reproducing achievement. For instance, pit settling birds, like woodpeckers and certain types of parrots, frequently face rivalry from obtrusive species like European Starlings and House Sparrows. These trespassers are known to assume control over tree holes, home boxes, or other appropriate settling areas, barring local species and possibly prompting decreases in their conceptive achievement.

b. Forceful Home Guard:
Some obtrusive bird species display forceful way of behaving, particularly during the reproducing season, which can additionally influence local birds. The presence of intrusive species like Normal Mynas or European Starlings might prompt expanded contest for settling destinations, with the intruders effectively safeguarding their domains against local species. This forceful way of behaving can dislodge local birds, restricting their reproducing open doors and adding to populace declines.

3. Contest for Food Assets:
a. Seed Predation and Scavenging Impedance:
Obtrusive species frequently rival local birds for food assets, especially in situations where their weight control plans cross-over. For instance, certain obtrusive species, similar to the Normal Myna, are known to be generalist feeders and deft foragers. They might consume natural products, seeds, or bugs that local birds additionally depend on, prompting expanded contest for these assets. Seed predation by obtrusive birds can affect the recovery of local plant species, disturbing the equilibrium of the environment.

b. Adjusted Rummaging Elements:
The presentation of obtrusive species can change the rummaging elements of local bird populaces. In regions where obtrusive birds rule, local species might be compelled to change their scrounging methodologies, moving to various food sources or adjusting their taking care of ways of behaving. These changes can have flowing impacts on the dispersion and wealth of both intrusive and local species, affecting the general design of the avian local area.

4. Illness Transmission:
Obtrusive species might go about as supplies for infections that can be communicated to local birds. This presents an extra layer of rivalry for assets, as the spread of illnesses can affect the wellbeing and endurance of local populaces. For instance, the presentation of obtrusive mosquitoes conveying avian jungle fever has been connected to decreases in local bird species in Hawaii. Local birds, not having advanced with these illnesses, may need invulnerability, making them more helpless to disease.

5. Influence on Island Biological systems:
Island biological systems, with their novel and frequently separated conditions, are especially helpless against the effects of obtrusive species. The presentation of non-local birds, vertebrates, or plants can prompt fast and extreme interruptions. Obtrusive species, liberated from regular hunters and contenders, can multiply and overwhelm island natural surroundings, frequently bringing about the downfall or termination of local species.

For instance, on islands where intrusive rodents have been presented, ground-settling birds face elevated predation pressure. The destruction or control of obtrusive species turns into a basic preservation methodology to safeguard local island bird populaces and reestablish environmental equilibrium.

6. Protection Difficulties and The board Techniques:
a. Coordinated Nuisance The board:
Preservationists utilize coordinated bother the executives systems to control obtrusive species and alleviate their effects on local bird populaces. This approach includes a mix of strategies like living space reclamation, evacuation of obtrusive people, and the execution of organic controls.

b. Rebuilding of Regular Hunters:
At times, once again introducing or advancing the presence of normal hunters that have some control over obtrusive species turns into a feasible preservation technique. For instance, the acquaintance of hunters like snakes with control obtrusive rodents on islands has been endeavored to reestablish harmony in biological systems.

c. Observing and Early Recognition:
Early discovery and checking of intrusive species are significant for successful preservation. Opportune distinguishing proof takes into consideration fast reaction measures, forestalling the foundation and spread of intrusive species before they hurt local bird populaces.

Chapter 5
Conservation Efforts

Preservation endeavors assume a critical part in shielding biodiversity, safeguarding biological systems, and guaranteeing the maintainability of our planet. As human exercises keep on applying remarkable tensions on the climate, the requirement for powerful protection measures has never been really squeezing. This thorough investigation digs into the assorted aspects of preservation endeavors, looking at the techniques utilized, the difficulties confronted, and the remarkable accomplishments in the continuous mission to protect the rich embroidery of life on The planet.

I. Figuring out Protection:
A. Definition and Goals:
Preservation, in the biological setting, alludes to the reasonable administration and assurance of normal assets, environments, and species. The essential goals of protection endeavors are to keep up with or reestablish the wellbeing and usefulness of environments, forestall the eradication of species, and advance the maintainable utilization of normal assets for current and people in the future.

B. Significance of Preservation:
Preservation is vital to keeping up with the equilibrium of biological systems, giving fundamental environment benefits, and safeguarding biodiversity. Biodiversity, the assortment of life on The planet, guarantees the versatility of environments, adds to human prosperity, and has characteristic worth. Protection endeavors are basic for alleviating the effects of living space misfortune, environmental change, contamination, and other anthropogenic tensions that undermine the fragile trap of life.

II. Protection Procedures:
A. Safeguarded Regions:

Public Stops and Holds: Assigning regions as public stops and saves safeguards regular natural surroundings and confines human exercises that might debase these conditions. These safeguarded regions act as shelters for different species and add to the preservation of hereditary variety.

Marine Safeguarded Regions: In marine conditions, laying out marine safeguarded regions (MPAs) is essential for defending marine biodiversity.

MPAs can assist with reestablishing fish populaces, safeguard coral reefs, and moderate the effects of overfishing.

B. Living space Reclamation:
Reforestation: Reforestation projects intend to reestablish debased or deforested regions by establishing local tree species. This sequesters carbon, forestall soil disintegration, and make living spaces for assorted vegetation.

Wetland Reclamation: Wetlands, indispensable for biodiversity and water sanitization, are many times debased by human exercises. Rebuilding endeavors include restoring normal hydrology, eliminating intrusive species, and establishing local vegetation.

C. Species Preservation:
Reproducing Projects: Hostage rearing projects center around reproducing and once again introducing jeopardized species into their regular natural surroundings. Zoos, aquariums, and specific offices assume a critical part in these projects.

Preservation Stores: Laying out preservation saves for explicit species, especially those in danger of eradication, gives a safeguarded climate where designated protection endeavors can be carried out.

D. Economical Asset The executives:
Timberland The executives: Carrying out economical logging rehearses assists balance the interest for wood items with the need to monitor backwoods environments. Affirmation frameworks, like FSC (Woods Stewardship Chamber), advance dependable ranger service.

Fisheries The board: Practical fisheries the executives includes setting get limits, safeguarding bringing forth grounds, and limiting bycatch. These actions mean to guarantee the drawn out feasibility of fish populaces.

E. Local area Based Protection:
Native and Neighborhood Association: Including native networks and nearby populaces in protection endeavors is fundamental. Customary biological information frequently supplements logical methodologies, and neighborhood networks become stewards of their normal assets.

Eco-the travel industry: Dependable eco-the travel industry can give monetary motivators to preservation. When overseen reasonably, eco-the travel industry can add to nearby economies while advancing the safeguarding of normal living spaces.

F. Environmental Change Alleviation:
Sustainable power Reception: Progressing to environmentally friendly power sources, for example, sun oriented and wind, lessens the dependence on petroleum derivatives, relieving environmental change and its effects on biological systems.

Carbon Sequestration Tasks: Drives pointed toward catching and putting away carbon, like afforestation and reforestation, add to environmental change moderation by lessening ozone harming substance fixations in the air.

III. Protection Difficulties:
A. Natural surroundings Misfortune and Fracture:
Urbanization: Fast urbanization prompts environment obliteration, as regular regions are changed over into metropolitan scenes. Discontinuity of environments makes it challenging for species to move, lessening hereditary variety and expanding the gamble of populace decline.

Farming Development: Huge scope horticulture frequently includes clearing timberlands and other normal environments. Monoculture practices can prompt biodiversity misfortune and the debasement of soil and water quality.

B. Overexploitation:
Overfishing: Impractical fishing works on, including overfishing and damaging fishing techniques, drain fish populaces and mischief marine environments. Tending to overfishing requires compelling fisheries the executives and authorization of guidelines.

Unlawful Untamed life Exchange: The unlawful exchange of untamed life, driven by interest for colorful pets, conventional drugs, and extravagance products, represents a huge danger to numerous species. Protection endeavors should incorporate measures to battle poaching and unlawful exchange.

C. Contamination:
Plastic Contamination: The expansion of plastic in seas and earthly conditions represents an extreme danger to natural life. Protection endeavors plan to decrease plastic utilization, work on squander the board, and address the main drivers of plastic contamination.

Compound Contamination: Pesticides, herbicides, and modern toxins can taint biological systems, influencing the strength of species and disturbing natural cycles. Executing and authorizing guidelines on substance use are fundamental for protection.

D. Environmental Change:
Increasing Temperatures: Environmental change is adjusting temperature designs, influencing the circulation and conduct of species. Protection methodologies should incorporate measures to assist species with adjusting to changing environments and decrease in general ozone harming substance emanations.

Ocean Level Ascent: Waterfront biological systems, home to different species, are undermined by rising ocean levels. Preservation endeavors center around securing and reestablishing waterfront living spaces, as well as anticipating oversaw retreat in weak regions.

E. Obtrusive Species:
Influence on Local Species: Obtrusive species can outcompete and disturb local biological systems. Protection endeavors include early identification, annihilation programs, and the reclamation of environments influenced by intrusive species.

Worldwide Development of Species: Expanded worldwide exchange and travel work with the unexpected acquaintance of intrusive species with new locales. Fortifying biosecurity measures is significant to forestalling the spread of invasives.

IV. Protection Examples of overcoming adversity:
A. Goliath Panda Preservation:
Endeavors to preserve the goliath panda in China have been strikingly fruitful. Through natural surroundings assurance, hostile to poaching measures, and local area inclusion, panda populaces have expanded. The panda's notorious status has likewise brought issues to light and financing for more extensive preservation drives in China.

B. Bald Eagle Recuperation:
The bald eagle, an image of the US, confronted an extreme downfall because of environment misfortune and the impacts of DDT, a pesticide. Preservation endeavors, including the forbidding of DDT, territory security, and hostage reproducing programs, prompted the recuperation of bald eagle populaces, bringing about their expulsion from the jeopardized species list.

C. Humpback Whale Protection:
Global participation and preservation endeavors have added to the recuperation of humpback whale populaces. Prohibitions on business whaling, safeguarded marine regions, and public mindfulness crusades have prompted huge expansions in humpback whale numbers in different sea districts.

D. African Elephant Preservation:
Preservation programs in Africa have zeroed in on fighting poaching and tending to human-elephant clashes. Safeguarded regions, against poaching watches, and local area based protection drives have added to the adjustment of some elephant populaces.

V. Future Headings in Protection:
A. Preservation Innovation:

Remote Detecting: Satellite innovation and remote detecting assume a urgent part in checking changes in biological systems, following deforestation, and evaluating the wellbeing of territories.

Protection Robots: Automated elevated vehicles (UAVs) or drones give a savvy and effective method for observing untamed life, living spaces, and implementation endeavors, especially in testing or far off conditions.

B. Engineered Science:
Progressions in manufactured science offer opportunities for protection, including quality altering strategies to relieve the effects of obtrusive species, address illness dangers, and improve the versatility of species even with ecological difficulties.

C. Coordinated effort and Global Collaboration:
Tending to worldwide preservation challenges requires cooperative endeavors on a global scale. Drives like the Show on Natural Variety (CBD) and the Unified Countries Feasible Advancement Objectives (SDGs) underline the significance of global participation in accomplishing protection goals.

D. Native Information Coordination:
Perceiving and integrating customary natural information held by native networks is fundamental for compelling protection. Native people group frequently have important bits of knowledge into neighborhood biological systems, biodiversity, and maintainable asset the board.

E. Environment Tough Preservation:
Protection techniques should progressively zero in on building versatility in biological systems and species to adapt to the effects of environmental change. This incorporates planning safeguarded regions and rebuilding projects that think about future environment situations and working with the relocation of species to adjust to evolving conditions.

5.1 Protected Areas and Wildlife Reserves

Safeguarded regions and untamed life holds are fundamental parts of worldwide preservation endeavors, filling in as safe-havens for different biological systems and the bunch species that possess them. These assigned regions assume a urgent part in saving biodiversity, keeping up with biological equilibrium, and shielding normal legacy for people in the future. In this investigation, we dig into the meaning of safeguarded regions and natural life saves, analyzing their jobs, challenges, and the significance of powerful administration in the continuous journey for protection.

Meaning of Safeguarded Regions:
1. Biodiversity Preservation:
Safeguarded regions are fundamental for preserving biodiversity by giving places of refuge to a wide cluster of plant and creature species. These regions act as shelters for imperiled and endemic species, offering them an opportunity to flourish and adding to the general wealth of worldwide biodiversity.

2. Natural surroundings Security:
One of the essential elements of safeguarded regions is to defend regular living spaces from human exercises that can prompt natural surroundings corruption and misfortune. By confining specific human mediations, like deforestation, mining, and urbanization, these regions assist with keeping up with the trustworthiness of environments and guarantee the endurance of different vegetation.

3. Biological system Administrations:
Safeguarded regions assume a key part in supporting fundamental biological system administrations. These administrations incorporate clean air and water, fertilization of harvests, environment guideline, and soil richness. By safeguarding unblemished biological systems, these regions add to the prosperity of both the climate and human social orders.

4. Logical Exploration and Training:
Safeguarded regions give significant open doors to logical examination and ecological instruction. Analysts utilize these regions as living research facilities to concentrate on normal cycles, screen species populaces, and better grasp environment elements. Furthermore, safeguarded regions act as open air study halls, teaching general society about the significance of protection and cultivating a feeling of stewardship for the climate.

Sorts of Safeguarded Regions:
1. Public Parks:
Public parks are assigned regions put away for the preservation of regular scenes and untamed life. These regions frequently focus on the safeguarding of perfect conditions, offering sporting open doors while keeping up with the environmental equilibrium. Models remember Yellowstone Public Park for the US and Serengeti Public Park in Tanzania.

2. Natural life Asylums and Stores:
Natural life safe-havens and stores center explicitly around the security of natural life. They give places of refuge to creatures to raise, feed, and move without critical human impedance. Kaziranga Public Park in India, known for its populace of Indian rhinoceroses, is an illustration of a natural life safe-haven.

3. Marine Safeguarded Regions:
Marine safeguarded regions (MPAs) are assigned zones in seas or oceans pointed toward saving marine environments and species. These regions can incorporate coral reefs, seagrass beds, and significant fish favorable places. The Incomparable Hindrance Reef Marine Park in Australia is a prestigious illustration of a marine safeguarded region.

4. Biosphere Stores:
Biosphere holds are regions assigned to accommodate the preservation of biodiversity with practical turn of events. They commonly incorporate center regions with severe preservation measures, cushion zones considering maintainable exercises, and progress regions where trial and error and finding out about reasonable practices happen. The Mananara-Nord Biosphere Hold in Madagascar represents this methodology.

5. World Legacy Destinations:
Assigned by UNESCO, World Legacy Destinations perceive areas of extraordinary social or normal importance. Numerous World Legacy Locales envelop both normal and social qualities, stressing the interconnectedness of human social orders and the climate. Yellowstone Public Park in the US is a double recorded site, perceived for its normal and social importance.

Challenges Looked by Safeguarded Regions:
1. Human-Natural life Struggle:
As human populaces infringe upon the lines of safeguarded regions, clashes among natural life and nearby networks frequently emerge. Issues, for example, crop striking by elephants, predation on domesticated animals, and assaults on people can prompt pessimistic impression of safeguarded regions and upset protection endeavors.

2. Poaching and Criminal operations:
Safeguarded regions are frequently focused on by poachers looking to benefit from the unlawful exchange of untamed life items, including ivory, rhino horns, and fascinating pets. Powerful insurance against poaching requires hearty policing, commitment, and global joint effort to battle natural life dealing.

3. Insufficient Subsidizing and Assets:
Many shielded regions experience the ill effects of lacking financing and assets, restricting their ability for powerful administration. Inadequate spending plans can think twice about exercises, for example, hostile to poaching watches, environment reclamation, and local area outreach programs.

4. Environmental Change Effects:
Environmental change represents a danger to the biological systems inside safeguarded regions. Climbing temperatures, adjusted precipitation examples, and more successive outrageous climate occasions can affect the appropriation of species, disturb movement examples, and lead to shifts in vegetation types. Preservation systems should integrate environment versatility measures to address these difficulties.

5. Discontinuity and Availability Issues:
Fracture of territories, frequently brought about by framework improvement and urbanization, represents a huge test to the viability of safeguarded regions. It can impede the development of natural life, disturb environmental cycles, and add to the deficiency of hereditary variety. Laying out untamed life hallways and upgrading network between safeguarded regions is fundamental for tending to this test.

The Significance of Successful Administration:
1. Implementation of Guidelines:
Successful administration of safeguarded regions requires the implementation of guidelines to forestall criminal operations like poaching, logging, and natural surroundings obliteration. Thoroughly prepared and prepared park officers assume a urgent part in watching safeguarded regions, dissuading criminal operations, and get-together information for protection endeavors.

2. Local area Commitment:

Drawing in neighborhood networks in the administration of safeguarded regions is fundamental for long haul achievement. Cooperative methodologies that include neighborhood occupants in dynamic cycles, offer elective livelihoods, and underscore the advantages of preservation add to a feeling of pride and shared liability regarding safeguarded regions.

3. Examination and Checking:

Ceaseless exploration and observing inside safeguarded regions are fundamental for figuring out biological system elements, following changes in species populaces, and assessing the adequacy of protection measures. Logical information guides versatile administration procedures and illuminates dynamic cycles.

4. Supportable The travel industry Practices:

Offsetting preservation objectives with supportable the travel industry is a sensitive yet fundamental part of successful administration. Appropriately oversaw the travel industry can create income for the support of safeguarded regions while bringing issues to light about the significance of biodiversity. In any case, unregulated the travel industry can prompt environment debasement and aggravation to untamed life.

5. Worldwide Cooperation:

Considering that numerous species and biological systems range different nations, global coordinated effort is urgent for the outcome of safeguarded regions. Shared preservation objectives, cooperative exploration drives, and composed endeavors to battle transboundary issues, for example, untamed life dealing add to the viability of safeguarded region the executives.

Examples of overcoming adversity in Safeguarded Region The board:
1. Costa Rica's Public Parks:

Costa Rica has turned into a worldwide forerunner in preservation by effectively dealing with its public stops and safeguarded regions. With a solid obligation to biodiversity protection, Costa Rica has switched deforestation patterns, expanded backwoods cover, and fostered a flourishing eco-the travel industry.

2. Yellowstone to Yukon Protection Drive:

The Yellowstone to Yukon Protection Drive centers around making and keeping up with availability for natural life across the tremendous district spreading over from Yellowstone Public Park in the U.S. to Canada's Yukon. By laying out untamed life halls and advancing reasonable land-use rehearses, the drive means to guarantee the drawn out practicality of assorted species.

3. Galápagos Islands Protection:

The Galápagos Islands, an UNESCO World Legacy Site, have executed severe preservation measures to safeguard the interesting vegetation of the archipelago. Hearty biosecurity measures, maintainable the travel industry practices, and dynamic local area inclusion add to the safeguarding of this famous biological system.

4. Bhutan's Preservation Achievement:

Bhutan, known for its obligation to Net Public Joy, has carried out protection arrangements implanted in social and ecological qualities. The country's broad safeguarded region organization, including public parks and untamed life asylums, has added to the preservation of jeopardized species like the snow panther.

Future Headings and Developments:
1. Protection Innovation:

Headways in innovation, including satellite symbolism, remote detecting, and man-made consciousness, are upsetting the observing and the executives of safeguarded regions. These apparatuses empower more effective information assortment, early location of dangers, and informed decision-production for preservation endeavors.

2. Native and Neighborhood Information Combination:

Perceiving and consolidating the conventional biological information on native networks is significant for compelling protection. Native people groups frequently have profound bits of knowledge into neighborhood biological systems, reasonable asset the executives practices, and versatility procedures that can improve protection drives.

3. Environment Strong Preservation:

Protection techniques should progressively zero in on building flexibility in environments and species to adapt to the effects of environmental change. This incorporates planning safeguarded regions and rebuilding projects that think about future environment situations and work with the movement of species to adjust to evolving conditions.

4. Supportable Funding Components:

Creating supportable funding components for safeguarded regions is fundamental for long haul achievement. This might include imaginative methodologies, for example, preservation finance, installment for biological system administrations, and organizations with private substances that perceive the worth of biodiversity.

5. Local area Based Protection Models:

Fortifying people group based preservation models includes enabling neighborhood networks to partake in and benefit from protection endeavors effectively. By adjusting preservation objectives to neighborhood interests, these models encourage a feeling of shared liability and add to the manageability of safeguarded regions.

5.2   Habitat Restoration Initiatives

Environment reclamation drives are fundamental parts of worldwide protection endeavors pointed toward moderating the effects of human exercises on biological systems and biodiversity. As human populaces grow and different anthropogenic tensions escalate, the debasement and loss of regular territories have become huge dangers to the wellbeing of our planet. Accordingly, rebuilding drives look to invert these patterns, restore biological systems, and give a help to endless animal types. This investigation digs into the significance of environment rebuilding, key systems utilized, and striking examples of overcoming adversity that feature the potential for positive natural change.

Significance of Environment Reclamation:
1. Biodiversity Preservation:
Territory reclamation assumes a crucial part in monitoring biodiversity by reproducing or upgrading reasonable conditions for a different scope of animal groups. Many plants and creatures are complicatedly connected to explicit living spaces, and their endurance relies upon the accessibility of these environments. Rebuilding endeavors intend to give places of refuge to compromised and jeopardized species, adding to the general extravagance of worldwide biodiversity.

2. Biological system Usefulness:
Reestablishing natural surroundings restores vital environmental cycles and works. Sound biological systems offer fundamental types of assistance like fertilization, water cleaning, and soil richness. By reestablishing debased natural surroundings, we upgrade the capacity of environments to support life, helping both natural life and human networks that rely upon these administrations.

3. Carbon Sequestration and Environmental Change Relief:
Reclamation drives add to environmental change relief by advancing carbon sequestration. Solid timberlands, wetlands, and different environments go about as carbon sinks, catching and putting away barometrical carbon dioxide. By reestablishing corrupted regions and establishing local vegetation, we can improve the limit of environments to retain and store carbon, subsequently assisting battle environment with evolving.
4. Versatility to Natural Changes:

Reestablished territories are in many cases stronger to natural changes, including environment variances and outrageous climate occasions. Different and well-working environments can all the more likely adjust to aggravations, making them more impervious to the effects of elements like dry seasons, floods, and intrusive species.

5. Sporting and Stylish Worth:
Reestablished territories upgrade the personal satisfaction for networks by giving sporting spaces and tasteful worth. Parks, wetlands, and green spaces made through rebuilding drives offer open doors for outside exercises, training, and an association with nature, adding to the prosperity of nearby occupants.

Key Systems in Natural surroundings Rebuilding Drives:
1. Reforestation:
Reforestation includes the replanting of trees in regions where timberlands have been drained or corrupted. This procedure reestablishes environment structure, further develop soil wellbeing, and give fundamental assets to different species. Effective reforestation projects frequently incorporate the utilization of local tree species to guarantee natural similarity.

2. Wetland Reclamation:
Wetland reclamation centers around restoring debased or depleted wetlands, which are basic environments for biodiversity and water guideline. Reclamation exercises might incorporate restoring regular hydrology, eliminating intrusive species, and establishing local vegetation. Very much reestablished wetlands give favorable places to sea-going species and add to water quality improvement.

3. Field and Grassland Rebuilding:
Meadow and grassland rebuilding endeavors expect to reproduce or improve local prairie biological systems. This includes establishing local grasses and forbs, controlling obtrusive species, and overseeing unsettling influences, for example, fire to mirror normal cycles. Reestablished prairies support a different cluster of natural life, including birds, bugs, and well evolved creatures.

4. Seaside and Marine Territory Rebuilding:
Seaside and marine territory rebuilding drives center around restoring corrupted coral reefs, seagrass beds, and mangrove backwoods. These biological systems offer fundamental types of assistance, including living space for marine species, coastline security, and backing for fisheries. Reclamation exercises might include coral transplantation, seagrass planting, and mangrove reforestation.
5. Metropolitan Greening and Brownfield Rebuilding:

In metropolitan regions, territory rebuilding drives frequently target debased or deserted destinations, known as brownfields. Metropolitan greening projects include changing these regions into green spaces, parks, or local area gardens. This upgrades biodiversity as well as works on the personal satisfaction for metropolitan occupants.

Examples of overcoming adversity in Territory Rebuilding:
1. Loess Level, China:
The Loess Level in China went through one of the biggest scene rebuilding projects on the planet. The region, once seriously debased by deforestation and unreasonable land use, was changed through afforestation, terracing, and soil protection measures. The undertaking not just superior the biological soundness of the area yet additionally helped nearby networks through expanded horticultural efficiency.

2. The Aral Ocean Delta, Kazakhstan and Uzbekistan:
The Aral Ocean, when one of the world's biggest inland oceans, experienced intense shrinkage because of water redirection for agribusiness. Endeavors to reestablish the Aral Ocean Delta included the development of dams, restoration of water stream, and the planting of vegetation. These drives have prompted the incomplete recuperation of the delta, bringing back a portion of the district's biodiversity.

3. Yucatan Promontory, Mexico:
The Yucatan Promontory confronted environment debasement and loss of biodiversity because of deforestation and unreasonable agrarian practices. Protection associations and nearby networks executed an enormous scope reclamation project, zeroing in on reforestation and economical land the board. This drive has added to the recuperation of biological systems and the assurance of jeopardized species.

4. The Netherlands:
The Netherlands has carried out broad wetland rebuilding ventures to address living space misfortune and further develop water the board. These endeavors incorporate the reclamation of peat swamps, making of new wetlands, and reconnection of waterways to floodplains. The reclamation exercises expect to improve water quality, forestall flooding, and give natural surroundings to different plant and creature species.

Challenges in Environment Rebuilding Drives:
1. Restricted Assets and Subsidizing:
Environment reclamation drives frequently face difficulties connected with restricted assets and subsidizing.

Rebuilding projects require monetary ventures for arranging, execution, and long haul checking. Getting financing and assets for supported endeavors can be an obstruction to the progress of rebuilding drives.

2. Obtrusive Species and Seed Obtaining:
The presence of obtrusive species can thwart reclamation endeavors by outcompeting local vegetation and disturbing biological system elements. Furthermore, obtaining suitable local seeds for reclamation activities can be testing, particularly in the event that the first seed bank has been exhausted or changed.

3. Environmental Change and Eccentric Biological system Reactions:
Environmental change brings vulnerabilities into living space reclamation drives. Modified precipitation designs, temperature changes, and outrageous climate occasions can affect the progress of rebuilding endeavors. Biological system reactions might be eccentric, requiring versatile administration methodologies.

4. Restricted Public Mindfulness and Commitment:
Fruitful environment rebuilding frequently depends on open mindfulness and local area commitment. Absence of mindfulness about the significance of reclamation, its advantages, and the way that people can contribute may upset the outcome of drives. Instructing and including nearby networks is fundamental for the drawn out maintainability of reclamation projects.

5. Strategy and Administrative Obstructions:
Strategy and administrative obstructions can block the advancement of natural surroundings reclamation drives. Now and again, clashing area use strategies, hazy guidelines, or regulatory obstacles might upset the execution of rebuilding projects. Smoothing out strategies and cultivating cooperation between partners can assist with beating these boundaries.

Future Bearings and Advancements:
1. Innovation Mix:
Progressions in innovation, like remote detecting, satellite symbolism, and geographic data frameworks (GIS), can upgrade the preparation and checking of territory rebuilding projects. These apparatuses give significant information to evaluating the viability of reclamation endeavors and distinguishing regions needing mediation.

2. Resident Science and Local area Inclusion:
Connecting with residents in logical information assortment and reclamation exercises through resident science drives upgrades local area contribution.

Nearby people group become dynamic members in the reclamation cycle, cultivating a feeling of responsibility and stewardship for reestablished living spaces.

3. Hereditary and Engineered Science:
Consolidating hereditary and engineered science approaches can support the improvement of plant and creature populaces with upgraded versatility to ecological stressors. This incorporates reproducing or designing species with characteristics that advance endurance in changing environments or debased conditions.

4. Scene Scale Reclamation:
Underscoring scene scale rebuilding approaches includes thinking about whole biological systems and their availability. This more extensive viewpoint considers the mix of different natural surroundings, working with the development of species and improving by and large biological versatility.

5. Roundabout Economy Standards:
Applying roundabout economy standards to environment rebuilding includes considering the whole life pattern of reclamation materials, limiting waste, and advancing practical asset use. This approach adjusts rebuilding drives to more extensive maintainability objectives.

5.3   International Collaboration for Bird Conservation
Global cooperation is vital for successful bird protection endeavors, taking into account the transitory idea of many bird species and the interconnectedness of environments across borders. Birds, frequently spreading over landmasses during their yearly relocations, rely upon living spaces that might be arranged in various nations. Cooperative drives, like peaceful accords, shows, and organizations, assume a pivotal part in tending to shared difficulties and guaranteeing the protection of avian biodiversity.

Key peaceful accords like the Show on Transient Species (CMS) and the Ramsar Show on Wetlands work with collaboration among nations to safeguard basic bird living spaces and advance reasonable administration. Cooperative examination tasks and observing projects include researchers and preservationists from various countries, considering a thorough comprehension of bird populaces and their environmental requirements. By sharing information, assets, and best practices, nations can cooperate to address dangers like territory misfortune, environmental change, and contamination, at last protecting the different and transitory bird species that improve biological systems worldwide. Global cooperation benefits birds as well as cultivates an aggregate obligation to saving the common regular legacy of our planet.

5.4 Citizen Science and Community Involvement

Resident science and local area contribution have arisen as integral assets in the domain of natural protection, including bird checking and biodiversity studies. Resident science connects with normal people in logical undertakings, changing them from detached onlookers into dynamic supporters of exploration and preservation endeavors. This participatory methodology not just extends the span and size of logical information assortment yet additionally encourages a feeling of association and obligation toward neighborhood environments.

With regards to bird protection, resident researchers frequently assume a significant part in bird observing projects. Equipped with optics and field guides, local area individuals contribute significant perceptions on bird species, conduct, and dissemination. Stages like eBird and BirdTrack permit people to present their bird sightings, making immense datasets that researchers use to follow populace patterns, movement designs, and the effects of natural changes.

Local area contribution stretches out past information assortment, enveloping living space reclamation, instructive drives, and support for bird-accommodating approaches. Neighborhood people group are exceptionally situated to grasp the complexities of their environments, and their dynamic commitment adds to a more exhaustive comprehension of the difficulties looked by bird populaces.

Besides, resident science ventures can engage people by encouraging a more profound association with nature and advancing ecological stewardship. As people group individuals witness the immediate effect of their endeavors on bird populaces and living spaces, a feeling of satisfaction and proprietorship creates, making a reasonable starting point for continuous preservation drives.

By joining the energy and information on nearby networks with the thoroughness of logical philosophies, resident science turns into an extension between different partners — researchers, preservationists, policymakers, and the overall population. This cooperative methodology represents the aggregate strength expected to address worldwide ecological difficulties and guarantee the drawn out wellbeing and variety of bird populaces and environments. Resident science stands as an information gathering system as well as an extraordinary power that democratizes logical request, making protection a common obligation and encouraging an agreeable connection among individuals and the normal world.

Chapter 6
Success Stories in Bird Conservation

Bird protection remains as a demonstration of mankind's capacity to switch the unfavorable effects of human exercises on the regular world. With living spaces disappearing and environmental change modifying biological systems, many bird species face the gamble of annihilation. In any case, in the midst of these difficulties, various examples of overcoming adversity in bird preservation rouse trust and underline the adequacy of devoted endeavors. This thorough investigation dives into a portion of these examples of overcoming adversity, inspecting the techniques utilized, the difficulties survive, and the more extensive ramifications for worldwide biodiversity.

1. The Bald Eagle's Resurgence

The Bald Eagle (Haliaeetus leucocephalus), when near the very edge of elimination, fills in as a momentous example of overcoming adversity in bird protection. During the twentieth 100 years, far and wide utilization of the pesticide DDT brought about slight eggshells, prompting regenerative disappointments among Bald Eagles. As a reaction, the US prohibited DDT in 1972, starting a sluggish however consistent recuperation for the species.

Preservation endeavors, including territory security, fake settling stages, and hostage reproducing programs, assumed a significant part in the Bald Eagle's resurgence. The species was eliminated from the jeopardized species list in 2007, denoting a victorious second for bird moderates. The Bald Eagle's recuperation not just features the significance of administrative activity in preservation yet in addition highlights the flexibility of nature whenever allowed the opportunity to recuperate.

2. The Peregrine Hawk's Re-visitation of Metropolitan Skies

The Peregrine Hawk (Falco peregrinus) is another avian example of overcoming adversity, especially in metropolitan conditions. Broad utilization of the pesticide DDT devastatingly affected Peregrine Hawk populaces, causing slender eggshells and conceptive disappointment. Like the Bald Eagle, the prohibiting of DDT contributed essentially to the species' recuperation.

Metropolitan conditions, once unfriendly to Peregrine Birds of prey, saw an astonishing resurgence. Peregrines adjusted to city life by using high rises and scaffolds as settling locales, going after pigeons and other metropolitan birds.

Moderates worked with this variation by introducing counterfeit settling destinations on structures. The Peregrine Hawk's flourishing presence in metropolitan scenes exhibits the versatility of untamed life and the potential for conjunction among people and untamed life.

3. The California Condor's Exceptional Rebound
The California Condor (Gymnogyps californianus) addresses a dazzling example of overcoming adversity in bird preservation, particularly taking into account it is the biggest flying bird in North America. By the late twentieth hundred years, the populace had plunged to a simple 27 people because of lead harming, natural surroundings obliteration, and poaching.
The California Condor's recuperation included a mix of hostage reproducing programs, lead ammo boycotts, and broad natural surroundings reclamation endeavors. In spite of confronting various difficulties, remembering the trouble of rearing condors for bondage, the species made a consistent recuperation. As of [latest year], the populace has expanded to over [current population], denoting a demonstration of the viability of cooperative preservation drives.

4. The Beating Crane's Excursion from Verge to Flight
The Outshining Crane (Grus Yankee folklore) is one of the most imperiled crane species internationally, with a turbulent history of close termination. By the 1940s, the populace had dwindled to only 16 people. Serious preservation endeavors followed, including hostage rearing, living space security, and the utilization of ultralight airplane to direct youthful cranes on their relocation courses.
The Outshining Crane's story highlights the significance of advancement in protection techniques. The utilization of ultralight airplane to show movement courses is a spearheading illustration of how innovation can support the recuperation of imperiled species. Today, the Beating Crane populace has expanded, and however challenges endure, the species fills in as an image of the potential for recuperation even notwithstanding serious danger.

5. Gooney bird Preservation: Moderating Dangers on Vast Oceans
Gooney birds, with their great wingspans, are glorious birds that meander the open seas. Be that as it may, they face critical dangers, essentially from fisheries. Numerous gooney bird species are inclined to bycatch, where they get trapped in fishing gear, prompting injury or passing. The Dark browed Gooney bird (Thalassarche melanophrys) is an eminent illustration of an animal varieties that has profited from designated protection endeavors.

Inventive measures, for example, the utilization of bird-startling lines and weighted snares, have been carried out to lessen bycatch. Also, global coordinated efforts have prompted the foundation of safeguarded regions in key taking care of and favorable places. The positive results of these endeavors are apparent in the balancing out or expanding populaces of some gooney bird species. The protection of gooney birds epitomizes the requirement for worldwide collaboration in shielding transitory species that cross huge breadths of the vast oceans.

6. The Kakapo: A Remarkable Protection Challenge

The Kakapo (igops habroptilus), a nighttime, flightless parrot local to New Zealand, presents an unmistakable and testing case in bird protection. By the 1990s, just 50 people remained, generally because of natural surroundings obliteration and predation by presented species. Preservationists started a serious recuperation program, including environment assurance, hunter control, and the utilization of advantageous taking care of to support reproducing achievement.

The Kakapo's story features the intricacies of saving species with one of a kind biological specialties. The bird's nighttime propensities and failure to fly make it particularly helpless against predation, requiring creative ways to deal with assurance. As of [current year], the Kakapo populace has expanded, exhibiting the viability of versatile preservation methodologies customized to the particular requirements of every species.

7. The Seychelles Songbird: Little Bird, Enormous Achievement

The Seychelles Lark (Acrocephalus sechellensis) is a little warbler that lives on a couple of granitic islands in the Seychelles. During the 1960s, the populace had dwindled to only 26 people because of territory annihilation and predation by presented species. A mix of environment rebuilding, intrusive species control, and movements to local islands added to the Seychelles Songbird's striking recuperation.

This example of overcoming adversity underlines the significance of island preservation, where confined and designated endeavors can significantly affect little populaces. The Seychelles Songbird's bounce back features the versatility of even the most basically jeopardized species when furnished with the essential help and mediations.

8. The Continuous Protection Adventure of the Amur Hawk

The Amur Bird of prey (Falco amurensis) embraces perhaps of the most unbelievable relocation, covering huge number of kilometers between favorable places in eastern Asia and wintering grounds in southern Africa. Regardless of its noteworthy perseverance, the species confronted a huge danger from boundless hunting in Nagaland, India, during its relocation.

Moderates, in a joint effort with nearby networks, started mindfulness crusades and attempted to control hunting through legitimate measures. The outcome of these endeavors is reflected in the uncommon decrease in hunting occurrences, permitting the Amur Bird of prey to proceed with its dazzling movement. This continuous adventure highlights the significance of local area association and worldwide coordinated effort in shielding species that navigate numerous nations during their life cycles.

6.1 Species Recovery Programs

Species recuperation programs address an encouraging sign in the domain of preservation, offering a life saver to living beings wavering near the precarious edge of eradication. As human exercises keep on modifying scenes, exhaust territories, and add to environmental change, numerous species face extraordinary difficulties. In any case, through purposeful endeavors, imaginative systems, and cooperative drives, species recuperation programs have demonstrated instrumental in reviving populaces and defending biodiversity. This investigation dives into the pith of species recuperation programs, analyzing their targets, challenges confronted, and striking examples of overcoming adversity.

Goals of Species Recuperation Projects

At their center, species recuperation programs expect to turn around the decay of jeopardized or basically imperiled species, cultivating their recuperation and possible expulsion from the edge of elimination. The essential goals incorporate living space reclamation, hostage rearing and renewed introduction, populace checking, and relieving dangers that prompted the species' downfall.

1. Living space Reclamation:

The underpinning of any fruitful species recuperation program lies in the rebuilding and protection of regular living spaces. Human exercises, going from deforestation to urbanization, frequently piece or annihilate territories essential for the endurance of numerous species. Environment reclamation includes recognizing key regions for protection, carrying out measures to lessen territory debasement, and, when possible, effectively reestablishing corrupted biological systems.

For example, on account of the California Condor recuperation program, living space reclamation assumed a urgent part. Endeavors zeroed in on securing and restoring the condor's local territories, guaranteeing they could flourish once again introduced into nature.

2. Hostage Reproducing and Renewed introduction:

Hostage reproducing programs are instrumental when an animal categories' wild populace is basically low.

In controlled conditions, for example, zoos or specific reproducing focuses, people are reared fully intent on delivering them into their normal living spaces once conditions are good. This methodology forestalls the total loss of an animal varieties while tending to dangers in nature.

The Bedouin Oryx gives a piercing model. Terminated in the wild by the mid 1970s, a hostage rearing project was started. Resulting fruitful renewed introductions into safeguarded regions in the Center East saw the species progressively recuperate, and by the 1990s, the Middle Eastern Oryx was downsized from "terminated in nature" to "jeopardized."

3. Populace Observing:

Thorough and continuous checking is crucial for evaluating the viability of protection endeavors. Populace checking includes following the numbers, ways of behaving, and strength of people inside an animal groups. This data measures the outcome of recuperation programs as well as illuminates versatile administration systems.

The Iberian Lynx recuperation program in Spain is a valid example. Through escalated checking, preservationists could distinguish patterns, survey the effect of dangers, and change systems as needs be. Subsequently, the Iberian Lynx populace, when nearly termination, encountered a slow increment.

4. Danger Moderation:

Tending to the main drivers of an animal types' downfall is vital. Dangers can go from territory annihilation and contamination to obtrusive species and poaching. Powerful species recuperation programs create and carry out procedures to alleviate these dangers, frequently requiring cooperation with neighborhood networks, states, and worldwide associations.

The Ocean Turtle Preservation Program fills in as a commendable case. By resolving issues like unlawful egg assortment, territory annihilation, and unintentional bycatch in fishing gear, the program has added to the recuperation of different ocean turtle species across the globe.

Challenges Looked by Species Recuperation Projects

While species recuperation programs have accomplished exceptional triumphs, they are not without challenges. The complexities of natural frameworks, the unusualness of human way of behaving, and the intricacy of elements adding to an animal varieties' decay present considerable snags.

1. Restricted Assets:

Numerous species recuperation programs work with restricted monetary assets and staff. The broad necessities of natural surroundings reclamation, continuous observing, and hostage reproducing request critical ventures. Contest for financing, especially when alluring or lead species gather more consideration, can leave less famous species neglected.

Endeavors to preserve less-referred to species, for example, certain creatures of land and water or bugs, face a daunting struggle in getting sufficient assets. The test lies in persuading partners regarding the significance of protecting biodiversity at all levels of the natural pyramid.

2. Absence of Public Mindfulness:

The progress of numerous species recuperation programs relies on open mindfulness and backing. Absence of understanding about the significance of biodiversity and the job of less popular species in biological system security can obstruct preservation endeavors. Also, charming megafauna frequently eclipse more modest, less breathtaking species concerning public consideration and financing.

Programs that draw in nearby networks in protection, for example, schooling drives or ecotourism adventures, can assist with overcoming this issue. Bringing issues to light about the interconnectedness of all species encourages a feeling of obligation and proprietorship among networks, indispensable for the drawn out progress of recuperation programs.

3. Environmental Change and Unusual Variables:

Environmental change acquaints a layer of unconventionality with species recuperation endeavors. Adjusted weather conditions, moving living spaces, and changes in food accessibility can upset painstakingly spread out plans. Species that were once secure in unambiguous districts might find those regions unsatisfactory because of environmental change, requiring versatile administration procedures.

The polar bear, for example, faces critical difficulties because of the liquefying of Icy ocean ice, affecting its hunting grounds and capacity to get to prey. Environment informed preservation techniques are progressively urgent for the outcome of recuperation programs even with an evolving environment.

4. Illness Elements:

Illness episodes can represent a serious danger to recuperating populaces, especially in hostage rearing projects. The grouping of people close by other people makes them helpless to the fast spread of sicknesses. The Tasmanian Villain Facial Cancer Illness fills in as a piercing model, undermining the endurance of this notable species notwithstanding serious protection endeavors.

Carrying out powerful illness checking and anticipation estimates inside hostage populaces is fundamental. Quarantine conventions, hereditary variety the executives, and investigation into infection safe people are essential parts of fruitful recuperation programs.

Examples of overcoming adversity in Species Recuperation Projects
1. The Dim Wolf:
The recuperation of the Dim Wolf (Canis lupus) in the US fills in as a demonstration of the likely progress of species recuperation programs. Once extirpated from a lot of its noteworthy reach, coordinated endeavors, including legitimate securities, natural surroundings rebuilding, and public mindfulness crusades, prompted the slow recuperation of wolf populaces in specific locales.
Renewed introduction programs in Yellowstone Public Park and focal Idaho assumed a significant part in reestablishing environmental equilibrium and decreasing overpopulation of prey species. The Dim Wolf's recuperation shows the significance of comprehensive methodologies that think about environmental associations and draw in different partners.

2. The Humpback Whale:
The Humpback Whale (Megaptera novaeangliae) gives a momentous illustration of global joint effort and preservation achievement. Pursued extremely close to annihilation for their lard and oil, worldwide endeavors prompted the ban on business whaling in 1986. Ensuing recuperation projects and preservation estimates brought about a huge bounce back of Humpback Whale populaces around the world.
The species' recuperation grandstands the force of global collaboration in tending to dangers that range across seas. It additionally underlines the significance of progressing endeavors to safeguard marine living spaces and relieve arising difficulties, for example, entrapment in fishing gear and the effects of environmental change.

3. The Brilliant Lion Tamarin:
The Brilliant Lion Tamarin (Leontopithecus rosalia) confronted serious natural surroundings misfortune in Brazil because of deforestation. Accordingly, a complete animal varieties recuperation program including hostage rearing, living space reclamation, and local area commitment was started. The renewed introduction of hostage reared people into reestablished natural surroundings permitted the Brilliant Lion Tamarin populace to bounce back, and the species was minimized from "imperiled" to "powerless."
This example of overcoming adversity features the significance of tending to both direct dangers and hidden causes, like living space annihilation. The association of nearby

networks in protection endeavors further highlights the meaning of building organizations for the drawn out progress of recuperation programs.

6.2   Reintroduction Programs and Their Outcomes

Renewed introduction programs address a basic part of protection endeavors, expecting to resuscitate populaces of species in their local living spaces after declines or extirpations. These projects, however perplexing and testing, have yielded critical triumphs, offering a brief look at trust for biodiversity preservation. This investigation digs into the elements of renewed introduction programs, their goals, philosophies, and the results that highlight their effect on reestablishing environmental equilibrium.

Goals of Renewed introduction Projects:
Populace Reclamation:

One of the essential goals of renewed introduction programs is to reestablish reasonable and self-supporting populaces of species in their regular natural surroundings. This is especially pivotal for species that have encountered critical downfalls because of elements like environment obliteration, overexploitation, or presented hunters.

Biological system Wellbeing:

Once again introducing an animal varieties into its local climate adds to the general wellbeing and equilibrium of environments. Numerous species assume essential parts in biological cycles, like fertilization, seed dispersal, and keeping up with prey-hunter connections. The shortfall of an animal groups can disturb these cycles, prompting flowing consequences for other greenery.

Hereditary Variety:

Little and disengaged populaces frequently experience the ill effects of diminished hereditary variety, making them more vulnerable to infections and ecological changes. Renewed introduction programs expect to increment hereditary variety by presenting people from hostage reproducing programs or other suitable populaces, advancing the drawn out strength of the species.

Instructive and Mindfulness Advantages:

Renewed introduction programs likewise offer instructive and mindfulness benefits, cultivating an association between the general population and protection endeavors. Drawing in nearby networks in the process upgrades comprehension of the significance of biodiversity and the fragile equilibrium inside environments.

Approaches of Renewed introduction:

Hostage Rearing:

Hostage rearing is a typical strategy in renewed introduction programs, particularly for species with basically low populaces. Zoos, particular reproducing focuses, or asylums house people for rearing. When a practical populace is laid out, people are steadily once again introduced into their normal living spaces.

Movements:

Movement includes moving people starting with one area then onto the next, either inside their current reach or to another reasonable natural surroundings. This strategy is frequently utilized for species confronting nearby extirpation or while laying out new populaces to improve hereditary variety.

Delicate Delivery:

Delicate delivery includes adjusting hostage reproduced people to their common habitat before complete delivery. This interaction diminishes the shock of progressing from imprisonment to the wild, improving the probability of endurance.

Local area Commitment:

Effective renewed introduction programs frequently include coordinated effort with neighborhood networks. Drawing in networks in the preservation cycle can prompt better security of environments and diminished dangers to once again introduced populaces, cultivating a feeling of shared liability.

Results of Renewed introduction Projects:

California Condor:

The California Condor (Gymnogyps californianus) renewed introduction program remains as a noteworthy achievement. By the late twentieth 100 years, the populace had dwindled to a simple 27 people because of lead harming, natural surroundings obliteration, and poaching. Serious preservation endeavors, including hostage rearing and territory rebuilding, prompted a consistent expansion in the populace. As of [current year], there are over [current population], denoting a victory for the preservation local area.

Dim Wolf in Yellowstone:

The renewed introduction of Dark Wolves (Canis lupus) into Yellowstone Public Park during the 1990s fills in as an exemplary illustration of the environmental advantages of renewed introduction. Wolves had been extirpated from the recreation area in the mid twentieth hundred years, prompting overpopulation of herbivores like elk.

The renewed introduction of wolves had flowing impacts, controlling elk populaces, changing their way of behaving, and helping vegetation and other untamed life. This comprehensive way to deal with biological system rebuilding features the interconnectedness of species inside a climate.

Red Kite in the UK:
The Red Kite (milvus) renewed introduction program in the Unified Realm has been a victory for raptor protection. When wiped out in Britain, the species was effectively once again introduced in the late twentieth hundred years. The populace has since thrived, and Red Kites can now be noticed rising above scenes where they were once missing. This achievement exhibits the potential for painstakingly arranged renewed introduction endeavors to restore species in their authentic reaches.

Dark footed Ferret:
The Dark footed Ferret (Mustela nigripes) looked close eradication during the 1980s, with the most recent wild populace diminishing to a couple of people. A hostage rearing system was started, and resulting renewed introductions into their local grassland territories have seen populaces gradually bounce back. However challenges stay, the Dark footed Ferret's story shows the significance of a complex methodology in reestablishing an animal groups to its regular habitat.

Challenges and Progressing Endeavors:
While numerous renewed introduction programs have made progress, challenges persevere. Issues, for example, environment corruption, environmental change, and human-natural life clashes require continuous consideration. Moreover, the drawn out progress of once again introduced populaces frequently depends on versatile administration procedures, kept observing, and the commitment of neighborhood networks.

6.3   Conservation Strategies That Work

Even with raising natural difficulties, successful preservation procedures are critical to defending biodiversity and protecting environments. Throughout the long term, various methodologies have been created and refined, exhibiting promising results in the domain of preservation. This investigation digs into preservation techniques that have demonstrated effective, underlining their flexibility, cooperative nature, and ability to resolve both nearby and worldwide ecological issues.

1. Natural surroundings Security and Reclamation:
The protection and reclamation of regular environments stand as major mainstays of effective preservation endeavors.

Laying out safeguarded regions, public parks, and natural life holds helps shield basic territories from damaging exercises like deforestation, urbanization, and modern turn of events. These regions act as safe-havens for different species, empowering them to flourish and keep up with practical populaces.

Moreover, territory rebuilding projects assume a critical part in switching the harm caused for biological systems. Reforestation drives, wetland reclamation, and endeavors to restore debased scenes add to the recuperation of biodiversity, upgrade biological system benefits, and relieve the effects of environmental change.

2. Supportable Asset The board:

Preserving biodiversity requires the economical administration of regular assets. Carrying out mindful practices in fisheries, ranger service, and horticulture keeps up with environmental equilibrium while addressing human necessities. Strategies, for example, feasible logging, biological system based fisheries the board, and agroforestry advance the amicable concurrence of human exercises and regular environments.

The reception of economical horticultural practices, like natural cultivating and permaculture, diminishes the ecological effect of food creation, mitigates environment annihilation, and supports soil wellbeing. By offsetting human requests with biological system versatility, these methodologies encourage a more economical and fair relationship with the climate.

3. Local area Based Preservation:

Connecting with nearby networks in preservation endeavors is vital to making long haul progress. Local area based preservation perceives the significance of native information and nearby practices in saving biodiversity. Cooperative drives that include networks in direction, training, and asset the board engage them as stewards of their current circumstance.

By adjusting preservation objectives to the necessities and goals of nearby networks, these techniques cultivate a feeling of pride and obligation. This approach improves the viability of protection programs as well as addresses financial issues, making a mutually beneficial situation for the two individuals and nature.

4. Against Poaching and Natural life Wrongdoing Anticipation:

Poaching and natural life dealing present extreme dangers to numerous species, driving them towards elimination. Fruitful preservation procedures integrate hearty enemy of poaching measures and drives to battle natural life wrongdoing. Expanded watching, the utilization of innovation for observing, and severe policing to decreasing the unlawful exchange untamed life items.

Global joint efforts, for example, the endeavors to battle the unlawful ivory exchange, exhibit the viability of composed activities. By tending to the interest for untamed life items, bringing issues to light, and reinforcing lawful structures, these techniques add to upsetting lawbreaker organizations and safeguarding imperiled species.

5. Environmental Change Moderation and Transformation:
Perceiving the interconnectedness of protection and environmental change, techniques that address the two issues at the same time are acquiring conspicuousness. Preservation endeavors that attention on environmental change moderation include safeguarding carbon-rich biological systems like timberlands and wetlands, which go about as carbon sinks. Also, drives to decrease ozone harming substance outflows, advance environmentally friendly power, and upgrade energy proficiency add to worldwide environment objectives.
Variation methodologies perceive the certainty of environmental change effects and mean to assist biological systems and species with adapting to evolving conditions. This might include establishing environment versatile living spaces, helping species relocation, and carrying out measures to safeguard weak biological systems.

6.4 Lessons Learned from Successful Initiatives
As preservation drives all over the planet endeavor to address the earnest difficulties presented by ecological corruption and biodiversity misfortune, there are important examples to be gathered from effective undertakings. These examples highlight the significance of versatile procedures, joint effort, and a comprehensive way to deal with accomplishing enduring positive results.

1. Coordinated effort is Critical:
Fruitful protection drives frequently underline joint effort among assorted partners, including legislatures, NGOs, neighborhood networks, and the confidential area. By encouraging organizations, sharing information, and pooling assets, these drives make an aggregate effect that rises above individual endeavors. The foundation of cooperative stages works with the trading of thoughts, advances shared liability, and use an assortment of skill to address complex preservation challenges.

2. Local area Commitment and Strengthening:
Drives that effectively connect with nearby networks and enable them as fundamental parts of protection endeavors will generally yield more manageable outcomes. Perceiving and regarding nearby information, customs, and necessities guarantees that protection techniques line up with the interests of those straightforwardly impacted by natural changes.

Engaged people group become important partners in defending environments, going about as caretakers of regular assets and adding to the drawn out progress of preservation drives.

3. Versatile Administration and Adaptability:
The capacity to adjust and develop in light of changing conditions is a sign of fruitful protection drives. Perceiving that environments are dynamic and dependent upon different stressors, versatile administration systems permit moderates to change their methodologies in light of continuous checking and criticism. This adaptability is significant in exploring vulnerabilities, answering arising dangers, and tweaking protection mediations for most extreme adequacy.

4. Comprehensive Methodologies:
Tending to preservation challenges requires an all encompassing comprehension of biological systems and the interconnectedness of species, natural surroundings, and human exercises. Effective drives frequently incorporate living space insurance, supportable asset the board, environmental change contemplations, and local area improvement into an extensive procedure. Perceiving the intricacy of environmental frameworks and embracing interdisciplinary methodologies guarantees a stronger and adjusted protection system.

5. Schooling and Mindfulness:
Protection drives that focus on schooling and mindfulness add to building a feeling of ecological stewardship among the more extensive public. By encouraging a comprehension of the worth of biodiversity, the results of ecological corruption, and the job people can play, these drives make an establishment for a culture of manageability. Educated and connected with networks are bound to help protection endeavors, impact strategy choices, and embrace supportable practices in their day to day routines.

6. Long haul Vision and Responsibility:
Effective preservation drives are portrayed by a drawn out vision and supported responsibility. Perceiving that positive results frequently call for investment, tolerance, and perseverance, these drives focus on the foundation of getting through preservation structures. Long haul responsibility is fundamental for the recuperation of species, the rebuilding of biological systems, and the development of a protection ethos that reaches out across ages.

Chapter 7
The Role of Birds in Ecotourism

Birds assume a diverse and significant part in ecotourism, adding to the allure of normal scenes and cultivating a more profound association among people and the climate. The charm of avian variety, ways of behaving, and environments has made birdwatching a conspicuous and developing specialty inside the more extensive ecotourism industry. This thorough investigation dives into the different components of the job of birds in ecotourism, analyzing their importance in monetary, environmental, and social settings.

Financial Meaning of Bird-based Ecotourism
1.1. Creating Income
Bird-based ecotourism fills in as a huge financial driver, drawing in fans, picture takers, and nature darlings from around the globe. Birdwatching visits, directed by experienced ornithologists and nearby aides, set out business open doors in frequently rustic or immature regions. Nearby economies benefit from the flood of sightseers who look for avian encounters, adding to the manageability of these networks.

1.2. Foundation Advancement
The interest for birdwatching encounters encourages the advancement of framework, including lodges, perception stages, and directed visit administrations. Neighborhood people group, perceiving the financial capability of bird-based ecotourism, frequently put resources into practical foundation to upgrade the general insight for guests while limiting ecological effects.

1.3. Protection Subsidizing
Extra charges, directed visit charges, and different uses by birdwatchers frequently contribute straightforwardly to preservation endeavors. Many bird-based ecotourism drives consolidate a preservation charge, which is diverted into natural surroundings security, untamed life checking, and local area based protection projects. This monetary help turns into a basic life saver for the safeguarding of bird species and their environments.

Natural Meaning of Birds in Ecotourism
2.1. Biodiversity Protection
Birdwatching, as a type of ecotourism, advances biodiversity protection by causing to notice the wealth and uniqueness of avian species. Famous birding objections frequently concur

with areas of high biodiversity, and the interest produced by birdwatchers can convert into expanded protection endeavors for the two birds and their territories.

2.2. Natural surroundings Conservation

Bird-based ecotourism can go about as a defensive safeguard for natural surroundings under danger. The financial worth got from birdwatching supports nearby networks and states to put resources into living space conservation, guaranteeing that critical regions for bird species are monitored against contending land utilizes.

2.3. Research Open doors

Birdwatchers and ecotourists frequently twofold as resident researchers, giving important information on bird populaces, ways of behaving, and circulation. This resident science part of bird-based ecotourism adds to logical examination, helping ornithologists and progressives in grasping bird nature and illuminating preservation methodologies.

Social Meaning of Birds in Ecotourism
3.1. Social Character

Birds hold social importance in numerous social orders, and bird-based ecotourism gives a stage to the protection and festivity of social personalities. Native people group frequently integrate customary birdwatching rehearses into ecotourism drives, sharing their insight into nearby avifauna and social stories with guests.

3.2. Instructive Worth

Birdwatching visits offer instructive open doors for the two local people and travelers. Interpretive aides give experiences into the natural significance of birds, their ways of behaving, and their parts in environments. This instructive part cultivates a feeling of ecological stewardship, empowering guests to appreciate and add to preservation endeavors.

3.3. Social Trade

Bird-based ecotourism works with social trade among guests and neighborhood networks. As vacationers draw in with the nearby lifestyle, including conventional bird-related rehearses, a shared comprehension and regard arise.
This trade benefits the two players, improving the movement experience and advancing culturally diverse appreciation.

Difficulties and Best Practices in Bird-based Ecotourism
4.1. Preservation Difficulties

In spite of its various advantages, bird-based ecotourism faces difficulties, including living space aggravation, expanded human-natural life collaborations, and possible adverse consequences on bird populaces. Finding some kind of harmony between the travel industry exercises and protection needs is pivotal to relieve these difficulties.

4.2. Best Practices

To guarantee the manageability of bird-based ecotourism, it is basic to take on accepted procedures. This incorporates limiting aggravation to settling and taking care of destinations, executing mindful the travel industry rules, and effectively including nearby networks in dynamic cycles. Practical the travel industry confirmations and rules add to keeping a fragile balance between monetary increases and natural conservation.

7.1   Economic Benefits of Birdwatching

Birdwatching, when thought about a specialty side interest, has developed into a flourishing industry with critical monetary ramifications. Past its sporting and instructive viewpoints, birdwatching has turned into a strong driver of monetary action, adding to neighborhood economies, work creation, and protection endeavors. This complete examination investigates the multi-layered financial advantages of birdwatching, looking at its part in the travel industry, the related foundation improvement, and the more extensive effect on biodiversity protection.

1. The travel industry Income and Occupation Creation
1.1. The Development of Birdwatching The travel industry

Birdwatching the travel industry has seen significant development as of late, determined by a rising interest in nature-based and practical travel encounters. Birdwatchers, otherwise called "birders," travel to different objections around the world, picking areas prestigious for their avian variety and one of a kind natural surroundings. This flood in birdwatching the travel industry converts into significant income for neighborhood economies.

1.2. Monetary Effect on Neighborhood People group

Neighborhood people group in bird-rich regions benefit altogether from birdwatching the travel industry. The inundation of birders creates income for facilities, cafés, transportation administrations, and nearby aides.
These direct financial commitments are much of the time joined by backhanded benefits, like expanded interest for painstaking work, neighborhood produce, and social encounters, enhancing the positive effect on the local area's by and large monetary prosperity.

1.3. Work Creation and Private venture Amazing open doors

The development of birdwatching the travel industry sets out business open doors in regions that may somehow or another battle financially. Nearby aides with aptitude in bird ID, conduct, and territories are popular, giving reasonable occupations. Furthermore, the requirement for transportation administrations, convenience, and food foundations adds to work creation and the advancement of independent ventures taking care of the necessities of birdwatching travelers.

1.4. Broadening the Travel industry Season
Birdwatching can add to expanding the travel industry season in specific locales. Birds are available over time, and committed birdwatchers will visit objections during off-top seasons to notice explicit species or witness transitory occasions. This expansion of the travel industry season assists networks with keeping a consistent progression of guests, lessening the effect of irregularity on nearby economies.

2. Foundation Improvement
2.1. Interest in Ecotourism Foundation
The monetary advantages of birdwatching reach out past quick the travel industry incomes to remember speculations for foundation improvement. Perceiving the financial potential, networks and states frequently put resources into ecotourism framework to upgrade the birdwatching experience. This might incorporate the development of bird stows away, perception pinnacles, and very much kept up with trails, establishing a more vivid and open climate for birders.

2.2. Convenience Offices and Conveniences
The interest for birdwatching encounters drives the improvement of convenience offices customized to the necessities of birders. Eco-accommodating cabins, birding resorts, and guesthouses arranged in closeness to bird-rich regions take special care of the inclinations of nature fans. This framework advancement improves the travel industry experience as well as lines up with reasonable works on, limiting the biological impression of guests.

2.3. Local area Contribution in Foundation Ventures
Viable foundation improvement includes coordinated effort with nearby networks. Drawing in local area individuals in the preparation and execution of activities guarantees that foundation lines up with neighborhood needs and jelly the trustworthiness of regular natural surroundings. This participatory methodology adds to a feeling of pride among local area individuals, encouraging long haul maintainability.

3. Preservation Subsidizing and Mindfulness
3.1. Preservation Charges and Commitments
Birdwatching the travel industry frequently integrates a preservation expense as a feature of visit bundles or extra charges to birding areas of interest. These expenses are coordinated

toward subsidizing preservation drives, territory reclamation, and the insurance of key birding locales. The income produced contributes straightforwardly to the safeguarding of biodiversity and the biological systems that draw in birdwatchers.

3.2. Resident Science and Information Assortment

Birdwatchers assume a vital part in resident science, contributing significant information to logical exploration and protection endeavors. The perceptions made by birders, frequently kept in committed stages or submitted to birding associations, add to observing bird populaces, recognizing patterns, and figuring out the effect of ecological changes. This resident science part of birdwatching cultivates a more profound association among lovers and protection drives.

3.3. Instructive and Mindfulness Drives

Birdwatching the travel industry offers an instructive stage, bringing issues to light about the significance of biodiversity, biological systems, and the requirement for protection. Interpretive aides and instructive projects give bits of knowledge into avian environment, ways of behaving, and the interconnectedness of species inside biological systems. This instructive part adds to a more extensive comprehension of natural issues and advances a feeling of obligation among birdwatchers.

4. Difficulties and Alleviation Methodologies

4.1. Adjusting Protection and The travel industry Tensions

While birdwatching the travel industry brings monetary advantages, it additionally presents difficulties connected with natural surroundings aggravation and expanded human-untamed life cooperations. Finding some kind of harmony between the financial increases and preservation needs is fundamental. Procedures, for example, laying out conveying capacities with regards to birding locales, executing mindful the travel industry rules, and advancing moral birdwatching rehearses assist with relieving these difficulties.

4.2. Practical The travel industry Affirmations

The reception of practical the travel industry affirmations and rules is significant for guaranteeing that birdwatching the travel industry lines up with preservation goals. Certificates like those given by the Worldwide Maintainable The travel industry Committee (GSTC) and BirdLife Global's Economical Birdwatching drive help recognize and advance objections that focus on supportability, protection, and local area commitment.

4.3. Local area Based Preservation Systems

Integrating nearby networks into protection methodologies is indispensable for the drawn out progress of birdwatching the travel industry. By including networks in dynamic cycles, setting out open doors for them to benefit straightforwardly from the travel industry, and encouraging a feeling of stewardship, preservation endeavors can acquire urgent help and add to the economical improvement of bird-rich districts.

7.2   Responsible Tourism and Bird Conservation

Mindful the travel industry, portrayed by moral and reasonable travel rehearses, has arisen as a core value in the travel industry. When applied to birdwatching, a specialty yet quickly developing portion of the movement area, capable the travel industry turns into a useful asset for bird protection. This far reaching investigation digs into the cooperative connection between dependable the travel industry and bird protection, inspecting the rules that support mindful birdwatching, the advantages for avian species and their living spaces, and methodologies for guaranteeing an amicable concurrence among birdwatchers and the padded occupants of our planet.

Dependable The travel industry in Birdwatching
1. Moral Contemplations

Dependable birdwatching starts with moral contemplations that focus on the prosperity of birds and their environments. This includes embracing a non-meddlesome methodology, regarding the regular ways of behaving of the birds, and keeping away from activities that could cause pressure or unsettling influence. Moral birdwatchers focus on the government assistance of the birds over catching the ideal photo or getting a very close view.

2. Living space Preservation

Mindful birdwatching lines up with living space preservation endeavors. Birders perceive that the endurance of bird species is unpredictably connected to the safeguarding of their regular living spaces.

Supporting and upholding for safeguarded regions, nature stores, and untamed life hallways turns into an indispensable piece of dependable birdwatching. This incorporates regarding assigned ways, keeping away from off-trail investigation, and shunning upsetting settling destinations.

3. Limiting Ecological Effect

Capable birdwatchers limit their natural effect by taking on eco-accommodating travel rehearses. This might include utilizing low-influence transportation, lessening waste, and picking facilities and visit administrators that focus on manageability. By embracing the standards of "leave no follow," birdwatchers add to the preservation of environments while partaking in their avian experiences.

4. Instruction and Mindfulness

A fundamental part of mindful birdwatching is instruction and mindfulness. Birdwatchers, as representatives for the regular world, assume a urgent part in teaching themselves as well as other people about the birds they notice. Grasping the environmental meaning of birds, their ways of behaving, and the dangers they face cultivates a more profound association with nature and a feeling of obligation for its conservation.

The Advantages of Capable Birdwatching for Preservation
1. Protection Subsidizing
Capable birdwatching frequently includes the installment of extra charges, directed visit charges, or commitments to preservation associations. These monetary commitments straightforwardly support preservation drives, territory reclamation, and the insurance of key birding destinations. The income produced turns into a critical wellspring of subsidizing for progressing endeavors to defend avian biodiversity.

2. Local area Inclusion
Mindful birdwatching empowers local area contribution in preservation endeavors. Nearby people group are vital to the outcome of birdwatching the travel industry, and mindful practices guarantee that their necessities and points of view are considered. Connecting with networks in dynamic cycles, setting out financial open doors, and cultivating a feeling of stewardship add to the supportability of bird-rich districts.

3. Reasonable Framework Improvement
The dependable the travel industry approach stresses reasonable framework advancement. Birdwatching the travel industry drives an interest for eco-accommodating convenience, very much planned perception stages, and painstakingly arranged trails.
By putting resources into practical framework, objections improve the birdwatching experience as well as limit the environmental impression of guests, guaranteeing a harmony among the travel industry and preservation.

4. Logical Commitments
Mindful birdwatchers frequently twofold as resident researchers, contributing significant information to logical examination. Perceptions recorded by birders, particularly in less-investigated areas, help ornithologists and specialists in figuring out bird populaces, ways of behaving, and dissemination. This resident science part of capable birdwatching improves the logical comprehension of avian environment.

Techniques for Guaranteeing Capable Birdwatching
1. Instruction and Understanding
Advancing mindful birdwatching starts with schooling and understanding. Visit administrators, guides, and birdwatchers themselves ought to focus on finding out about the birds they

notice, the natural surroundings they visit, and the expected effects of their presence. Interpretive projects and instructive materials improve the comprehension of dependable practices and biological standards.

2. Set of rules
Laying out and advancing a set of rules is fundamental for directing birdwatchers in capable practices. This code might remember rules for avoiding birds, keeping away from playback of bird calls, and complying to assigned ways. Conveying and imparting this code helps set clear assumptions for mindful way of behaving.

3. Nearby Commitment and Strengthening
Nearby people group ought to be effectively drawn in and enabled in the turn of events and the board of birdwatching the travel industry. Including people group individuals in dynamic cycles, giving preparation and business potential open doors, and cultivating social trade add to a feeling of pride and shared liability regarding protection.

4. Observing and Guideline
Compelling checking and guideline are essential for guaranteeing that birdwatching the travel industry stays mindful. This might include laying out guest amounts for delicate regions, carrying out grant frameworks, and utilizing nearby screens to guarantee consistence with moral rules. Customary evaluations and acclimations to the executives techniques help address developing difficulties.

5. Coordinated effort and Systems administration
Mindful birdwatching benefits from coordinated effort and systems administration among partners. This incorporates coordinated effort between visit administrators, preservation associations, neighborhood networks, and legislative bodies. Sharing accepted procedures, planning endeavors, and taking part in territorial or worldwide organizations add to the aggregate effect of dependable birdwatching drives.

Difficulties and Future Contemplations
1. Adjusting Preservation and The travel industry Tensions
One of the essential difficulties is adjusting the financial advantages of birdwatching the travel industry with the protection needs of bird species and their living spaces. The rising ubiquity of birdwatching can prompt raised the travel industry pressures, requiring cautious administration to forestall adverse consequences on bird populaces.

2. Tending to Framework Improvement

While maintainable foundation improvement is a positive part of capable birdwatching, it likewise presents difficulties. The development of perception stages, trails, and facilities should be painstakingly intended to limit aggravation to regular natural surroundings. Also, overseeing guest stream and implementing rules become essential for forestalling environment corruption.

3. Empowering Dependable Way of behaving

Guaranteeing that birdwatchers stick to dependable practices requires continuous endeavors in training and mindfulness. Some birdwatchers may not know about the likely effect of their activities, stressing the requirement for nonstop correspondence, understanding projects, and the spread of dependable birdwatching rules.

4. Worldwide Consistency in Principles

As birdwatching the travel industry is a worldwide action, accomplishing consistency in dependable guidelines becomes fundamental. While territorial and nearby endeavors are vital, adjusting worldwide norms for capable birdwatching can add to a brought together methodology. Laying out global rules that regard social and natural variety can direct birdwatchers around the world.

7.3   Community Engagement in Ecotourism

Ecotourism, described by capable travel to regular regions that saves the climate and advances the prosperity of nearby networks, places local area commitment at its center. The progress of ecotourism is characteristically connected to the contribution of neighborhood networks, who are has as well as dynamic members in the preservation and the travel industry exercises. This extensive investigation dives into the diverse parts of local area commitment in ecotourism, looking at its importance, advantages, difficulties, and methodologies for cultivating maintainable associations.

The Meaning of Local area Commitment in Ecotourism
1. Protection Stewardship

Local area commitment in ecotourism lays out neighborhood networks as stewards of their common habitats. By including them in the preparation, navigation, and execution of ecotourism drives, there is a common obligation regarding the preservation of biodiversity and the security of delicate environments. This stewardship guarantees that the normal assets on which ecotourism depends are economically made due.

2. Social Safeguarding and Sharing

Neighborhood people group frequently have interesting social information and customs that add to the wealth of the ecotourism experience.

Connecting with these networks takes into account the conservation of social legacy and gives a legitimate experience to vacationers. The sharing of social works on, narrating, and conventional information makes a more significant and vivid experience for guests.

3. Financial Open doors
Ecotourism can possibly create critical financial open doors for nearby networks. By partaking in the travel industry related exercises, like directed visits, workmanship creation, and accommodation administrations, local area individuals can enhance their types of revenue. This financial strengthening is a vital driver in further developing jobs and decreasing reliance on unreasonable practices.

4. Upgraded Natural Mindfulness
Drawing in nearby networks in ecotourism adds to expanded ecological mindfulness. As people group individuals become ministers for their regular environmental elements, they gain a more profound comprehension of the significance of protection. This mindfulness, thusly, can prompt more feasible practices inside the local area and a more prominent deep satisfaction in their job as caretakers of the climate.

Advantages of Local area Commitment in Ecotourism
1. Long haul Supportability
Local area commitment is fundamental to the drawn out maintainability of ecotourism drives. At the point when nearby networks are effectively involved, there is a personal stake in the achievement and continuation of ecotourism projects. This makes a pattern of supportability where both the regular habitat and the local area's prosperity are reliant together.

2. Positive The travel industry Encounters
Local area commitment upgrades the nature of the travel industry experience. Guests frequently look for true collaborations and a more profound association with the spots they visit. Drawing in with nearby networks permits travelers to acquire bits of knowledge into the way of life, customs, and day to day existence of the objective, making really advancing and essential encounters.

3. Social and Social Advantages
The social and social advantages of local area commitment in ecotourism are critical. The travel industry can act as an extension for social trade, encouraging comprehension and appreciation among guests and local area individuals. This cooperation helps separate generalizations and advances a more comprehensive and interconnected worldwide local area.

4. Protection Results

Networks participated in ecotourism frequently assume a urgent part in protection results. Their firsthand information on neighborhood biological systems and untamed life, joined with a common obligation to economical practices, adds to the insurance of normal assets. Local area drove protection drives can be more powerful and versatile to nearby settings.

Challenges in Local area Commitment in Ecotourism
1. Power Elements and Value

Power elements inside the ecotourism business can present difficulties to significant local area commitment. Lopsided characteristics in dynamic power, benefit-sharing, and portrayal can prompt discriminatory results. Tending to these power elements is vital for cultivating real associations.

2. Social Responsiveness and Regard

Keeping up with social awareness and regard is a continuous test in local area commitment. Vacationers and administrators should know about social standards, customs, and holy destinations. Improper way of behaving or negligence for nearby traditions can strain connections and adversely influence the local area's view of the travel industry.

3. Adjusting Financial Advantages

While ecotourism can bring monetary advantages, there is a sensitive equilibrium to strike. Networks might confront difficulties in overseeing expanded appearance without undermining their social uprightness or the regular habitat. Finding some kind of harmony between financial increases and ecological and social protection requires cautious preparation.

4. Reliance on The travel industry

Networks vigorously subject to the travel industry might confront weaknesses, particularly during financial slumps or disturbances like the worldwide pandemic. Overreliance on the travel industry can make networks powerless to outside shocks, underlining the significance of enhancing work choices and building strength.

Systems for Encouraging Practical People group Commitment in Ecotourism
1. Comprehensive Dynamic Cycles

Guarantee that dynamic cycles are comprehensive and include the dynamic cooperation of local area individuals. This incorporates conferences, studios, and organizations that enable networks to add to the preparation and the executives of ecotourism drives.

2. Limit Building and Preparing

Put resources into limit building and preparing projects to improve the abilities of local area individuals associated with ecotourism.

This remembers preparing for directing, neighborliness, and supportable practices. Outfitting people group with the fundamental abilities guarantees a better of administration and upgrades the general guest experience.

3. Social Responsiveness Preparing for Sightseers

Execute social awareness preparing for travelers to advance conscious and mindful way of behaving. Visit administrators can assume a vital part in teaching guests about nearby traditions, customs, and the significance of limiting their effect on the local area and climate.

4. Broadening of Monetary Exercises

Support the broadening of financial exercises inside networks. This might incorporate supporting drives connected with agro-the travel industry, customary painstaking work, and other maintainable occupation choices. Broadening lessens reliance on a solitary pay source and improves local area versatility.

5. Benefit-Sharing Systems

Lay out straightforward advantage sharing systems that guarantee a fair dispersion of financial advantages among local area individuals. This might include income sharing arrangements, local area improvement reserves, or different components that straightforwardly add to the prosperity of the local area.

6. Ecological Schooling Projects

Carry out natural training programs inside networks to upgrade mindfulness about the environmental significance of their environmental elements. This schooling engages networks to effectively partake in protection endeavors and take on reasonable practices in their day to day routines.

7. Cooperative Associations

Encourage cooperative associations between networks, government offices, non-benefit associations, and confidential area elements. These organizations can use different aptitude, assets, and viewpoints to make all encompassing and practical ecotourism drives.

Contextual analyses: Effective Models of Local area Commitment in Ecotourism
1. The Maasai Mara Conservancies, Kenya

The Maasai Mara Conservancies in Kenya embody effective local area commitment in ecotourism. Nearby Maasai people group own and oversee conservancies, getting immediate monetary advantages from the travel industry. Income sharing arrangements, local area possessed cabins, and work valuable open doors for local area individuals have added to preservation results and further developed jobs.

2. Local area Based The travel industry in the Amazon, Peru

In the Amazon rainforest of Peru, people group based the travel industry drives engage native networks to share their social legacy and regular assets with guests. Neighborhood guides lead eco-accommodating visits, giving bits of knowledge into customary practices and the rich biodiversity of the district. Income produced upholds local area improvement and preservation endeavors.

3. Anangu People group Venture, Ecuador

The Anangu People group Venture in the Ecuadorian Amazon exhibits a reasonable model of local area commitment in ecotourism. The Anangu Kichwa people group works lodges, directed visits, and social encounters for guests. Through these drives, the local area creates pay, protects their social character, and effectively partakes in rainforest preservation.

Chapter 8
Future Challenges and Opportunities

What's in store is a steadily developing scene formed by a bunch of difficulties and open doors spreading over different spaces like innovation, climate, society, and financial matters. As we stand on the incline of what lies ahead, it is pivotal to expect, comprehend, and answer the powers that will shape our aggregate fate. This broad investigation digs into the diverse difficulties and open doors that loom not too far off, offering bits of knowledge into how people, networks, and countries can explore the intricacies representing things to come.

I. Mechanical Scene: It The upcoming Scene to Shape
A. Challenges in Innovation

1. Moral Ramifications of Man-made reasoning (artificial intelligence)
As man-made intelligence keeps on progressing, moral contemplations encompassing its utilization become foremost. Issues like predisposition in calculations, work removal, and the potential for abuse present difficulties that require smart guideline and moral systems to guarantee man-made intelligence benefits humankind without compromising central qualities.

2. Online protection Dangers
The rising dependence on advanced foundation uncovered social orders and people to network safety dangers. As innovation advances, so do the strategies for digital assaults. Fortifying online protection measures and encouraging worldwide participation are significant to shielding delicate data and basic frameworks.

3. Protection Concerns
The omnipresence of information assortment and reconnaissance advances raises worries about individual security. Finding some kind of harmony between mechanical development and safeguarding individual security is a continuous test that requires straightforward arrangements and powerful legitimate systems.

B. Amazing open doors in Innovation
1. Manageable Innovation Arrangements

Arising advances present chances to address squeezing worldwide difficulties, for example, environmental change and asset exhaustion. Manageable innovation arrangements, including environmentally friendly power developments, eco-accommodating assembling cycles, and round economy rehearses, offer pathways toward a more maintainable future.

2. Headways in Medical care

Mechanical headways in medical services, including customized medication, telehealth, and information driven diagnostics, can possibly change medical care conveyance. These advancements can upgrade availability, work on persistent results, and add to more productive medical care frameworks all around the world.

3. Network and Worldwide Coordinated effort

Upgraded availability through advances like 5G and past encourages worldwide joint effort. The capacity to share information, team up on examination, and address worldwide difficulties all in all is an open door that can drive positive change on a phenomenal scale.

II. Ecological Elements: Supporting the Planet for People in the future
A. Challenges in the Climate

1. Environmental Change Emergency

The raising effects of environmental change, including increasing temperatures, outrageous climate occasions, and biodiversity misfortune, represent an impressive test. Moderating environmental change requires critical worldwide activity, maintainable practices, and a progress to sustainable power sources.

2. Asset Shortage

Exhausting normal assets, including water, arable land, and minerals, present difficulties for future supportability. Taking on round economy standards, advancing asset proficiency, and investigating elective sources are basic for tending to asset shortage.

3. Loss of Biodiversity

The speeding up loss of biodiversity undermines environments and undermines their strength. Protection endeavors, manageable land use practices, and strategies that focus on biodiversity conservation are fundamental for keeping up with the strength of our planet.

B. Valuable open doors in the Climate
1. Sustainable power Change
The progress to sustainable power sources, for example, sun oriented and wind power, presents a huge chance for moderating environmental change. Putting resources into clean energy advancements and foundation can drive monetary development while decreasing dependence on petroleum derivatives.

2. Protection and Reclamation Drives
Worldwide drives zeroed in on protection and environment rebuilding can assist with switching biodiversity misfortune. Reforestation, marine protection, and economical horticulture rehearses add to the conservation and reclamation of biological systems.

3. Roundabout Economy Practices
Taking on round economy rehearses, which focus on the reuse and reusing of materials, offers a valuable chance to lessen asset utilization and waste. Round economy models can add to a more reasonable and strong worldwide economy.

III. Cultural Wildernesses: Forming Comprehensive and Fair People group
A. Challenges In the public arena

1. Social Disparity and Shamefulness
Persevering social imbalances in light of elements like race, orientation, and financial status keep on being critical difficulties. Resolving foundational issues, advancing inclusivity, and propelling civil rights are basic for building fair social orders.

2. Worldwide Wellbeing Emergencies
The continuous and future wellbeing emergencies, exemplified by occasions like the Coronavirus pandemic, present difficulties to medical care frameworks, social designs, and monetary strength. Fortifying worldwide wellbeing framework, further developing medical services availability, and it are critical to improve readiness.

3. Instructive Abberations
Abberations in admittance to quality training persevere worldwide. Crossing over the instructive hole requires interests in comprehensive training, utilizing innovation for remote learning, and addressing foundational boundaries to instructive open doors.

B. Open doors In the public arena
1. Variety and Consideration

Encouraging variety and consideration in all parts of society presents a chance for aggregate development and advancement.
Embracing assorted viewpoints, destroying fundamental predispositions, and elevating equivalent open doors add to additional dynamic and strong networks.

2. Mechanical Strengthening
The democratization of innovation gives open doors to strengthening, especially in underestimated networks. Admittance to computerized apparatuses, data, and online stages can enhance voices, set out financial open doors, and extension cultural holes.

3. Social Advancement and Business
Social advancement and business venture offer roads for tending to cultural difficulties. Arrangements that join business sharpness with social and ecological effect can drive positive change and add to manageable turn of events.

IV. Monetary Real factors: Exploring the Way to Thriving
A. Challenges in the Economy

1. Monetary Disparity
Developing monetary disparity presents dangers to social union and soundness. Tending to this challenge requires strategies that advance fair abundance appropriation, admittance to financial open doors, and social security nets.

2. Mechanical Joblessness
Progressions in robotization and man-made brainpower raise worries about work uprooting. Setting up the labor force for the future, encouraging reskilling and upskilling programs, and reconsidering work markets are fundamental for alleviating the effect of mechanical joblessness.

3. Worldwide Financial Vulnerabilities
The interconnectedness of the worldwide economy opens countries to monetary vulnerabilities, including monetary emergencies and international pressures. Fortifying global participation, differentiating monetary conditions, and it are fundamental to execute strong financial strategies.

B. Potential open doors in the Economy
1. Manageable Monetary Models
Changing to reasonable monetary models, like the roundabout economy and green money, gives open doors for adjusting financial development ecological and social

contemplations. Interests in clean energy, manageable agribusiness, and eco-accommodating businesses can drive thriving.

2. Computerized Change and Advancement
Embracing computerized change and cultivating development can spike financial development. Countries and organizations that put resources into innovation, innovative work, and advanced framework are better situated to adjust to changing monetary scenes.

3. Comprehensive Financial Turn of events
Focusing on comprehensive financial improvement guarantees that the advantages of development arrive at all fragments of society. Strategies that advance little and medium-sized ventures, support minimized networks, and diminish monetary inconsistencies add to stronger and reasonable economies.

8.1   Emerging Threats to Bird Populations
Bird populaces, necessary parts of biological systems all over the planet, are confronting a variety of arising dangers that risk their endurance. As human exercises and ecological changes speed up, the difficulties going up against bird species have become more intricate and different. This thorough investigation dives into the arising dangers to bird populaces, incorporating elements, for example, territory misfortune, environmental change, contamination, and illness. Understanding these dangers is vital for planning successful preservation methodologies and guaranteeing the drawn out endurance of avian biodiversity.

1. Environment Misfortune and Fracture
1.1. Urbanization and Framework Improvement
One of the essential dangers to bird populaces is the continuous extension of metropolitan regions and framework improvement. As urban communities develop and scenes change, regular environments are divided and supplanted by structures, streets, and different designs. This deficiency of natural surroundings upsets rearing, searching, and transient examples, influencing bird populaces that depend on unambiguous environments.

1.2. Rural Escalation
Serious farming works on, including the utilization of huge scope monocultures and pesticides, add to living space misfortune and debasement. The change of assorted regular scenes into uniform rural fields decreases the accessibility of reasonable natural surroundings for the overwhelming majority bird species. Pesticides and manures further posture direct dangers to birds through tainting of food sources and water.

1.3. Deforestation

Deforestation, driven by logging, horticulture, and other human exercises, is a huge danger to bird populaces, especially those in tropical rainforests. The deficiency of trees takes out settling destinations as well as upsets complex woods environments, influencing the bugs and organic products that birds rely upon for food.

1.4. Fracture and Segregation

Natural surroundings fracture secludes populaces and lessens hereditary variety among bird species. Segregated populaces are more defenseless against dangers, for example, infections and environment changes. Divided environments likewise prevent the normal developments and movements of birds, prompting populace declines and expanded weakness to different dangers.

2. Environmental Change Effects
2.1. Adjusted Relocation Examples

Environmental change is upsetting customary movement examples of many bird species. Changes in temperature and weather conditions influence the accessibility of food assets along movement courses. Birds might confront confuses in timing, with the pinnacle accessibility of bugs or blossoming plants as of now not synchronized with their appearance.

2.2. Changes in Reproducing Seasons

Increasing temperatures and adjusted occasional examples influence the planning of rearing seasons for birds. Changes in temperature and precipitation can influence the accessibility of food assets during basic times of proliferation, prompting diminished rearing achievement and populace declines.

2.3. Ocean Level Ascent and Waterfront Territories

Rising ocean levels, a result of environmental change, represent a danger to waterfront natural surroundings that many bird species depend on for rearing and taking care of. Seaside disintegration, saltwater interruption, and changes in vegetation can diminish the appropriateness of these region, affecting the endurance of species like shorebirds and seabirds.

2.4. Outrageous Climate Occasions

The recurrence and power of outrageous climate occasions, like storms and rapidly spreading fires, are on the ascent because of environmental change. These occasions can straightforwardly influence bird populaces by obliterating environments, causing home disappointments, and prompting expanded mortality. Species that are now in danger or have specific environment necessities are especially defenseless.

3. Contamination and Impurities

3.1. Pesticides and Rural Synthetics

The utilization of pesticides and rural synthetics represents an immediate danger to bird populaces. Insect poisons and herbicides can sully food sources, prompting harming of birds. Furthermore, the downfall of bug populaces because of pesticide use influences insectivorous birds that depend on them for food.

3.2. Plastic Contamination

The unavoidable issue of plastic contamination adversely affects bird species. Birds might ingest plastic particles, prompting inside wounds, blockages, and lack of healthy sustenance. Plastic flotsam and jetsam additionally presents ensnarement gambles, influencing seabirds and waterfowl specifically.

3.3. Air and Water Contamination

Air and water contamination from modern exercises, vehicle outflows, and ill-advised garbage removal influence bird territories and can prompt harmful consequences for bird species. Tainted water sources influence the accessibility of clean drinking water, while dirtied air can add to respiratory issues in birds.

3.4. Lead Harming

Lead harming, frequently coming about because of the ingestion of toxic ammo or fishing supplies, stays a critical danger to bird populaces. Ruthless birds, like hawks and vultures, are especially vulnerable. Ingested lead can cause neurologic and stomach related issues, prompting mortality.

4. Infection and Arising Microbes

4.1. Avian Flu and Other Viral Infections

Avian flu and other viral infections can devastatingly affect bird populaces. Flare-ups of these illnesses can prompt mass mortalities, especially in thickly populated regions or in areas where birds gather during relocation. The transmission of infections among wild and tamed birds further compounds the danger.

4.2. Parasitic Diseases

Parasites, like vermin, lice, and ticks, can overrun bird populaces, causing a scope of medical problems. Notwithstanding immediate mischief, parasitic diseases can prompt diminished regenerative achievement, influencing the general populace elements of bird species.

4.3. Arising Untamed life Infections

The development of new and inadequately comprehended untamed life illnesses represents a danger to bird populaces. Environmental change, territory obliteration, and expanded human-natural life connections can add to the spread of novel microorganisms, endangering weak bird species.

4.4. Vector-Borne Illnesses

Illnesses sent by vectors, like mosquitoes and ticks, can influence bird populaces. The extension of vector living spaces because of environmental change, alongside worldwide travel and exchange, builds the gamble of bird-to-bird transmission and the acquaintance of new infections with various locales.

5. Intrusive Species and Predation
5.1. Predation by Intrusive Species

The acquaintance of non-local species with new conditions can bring about predation pressures on local bird populaces. Intrusive hunters, like rodents, felines, and snakes, can pulverize neighborhood bird species that poor person advanced guards against these presented dangers.

5.2. Contest for Assets

Obtrusive plant species can outcompete local vegetation, adjusting territories and influencing the accessibility of food assets for birds. Changes in vegetation design and sythesis can prompt decreases in bird populaces that rely upon explicit plant species for settling, searching, or cover.

5.3. Hybridization and Hereditary Dangers

The presentation of non-local species can prompt hybridization with local species, bringing about hereditary dangers. Hybridization can weaken the hereditary honesty of local populaces, possibly prompting diminished wellness and flexibility.

6. Human Aggravation and Double-dealing
6.1. Sporting Exercises and The travel industry

Human sporting exercises, including birdwatching, climbing, and sailing, can upset settling and taking care of ways of behaving of bird species. Elevated degrees of aggravation can prompt deserted homes, focused people, and decreased regenerative achievement.

6.2. Unlawful Exchange and Double-dealing

The unlawful exchange of birds for the pet business, conventional medication, and different purposes stays a danger to numerous animal groups.

The catch and exchange of birds, particularly those with lively plumage or special attributes, can prompt populace declines and disturb regular biological systems.

6.3. Overharvesting and Hunting

Overharvesting of bird species for food, feathers, or different items can have extreme ramifications for populaces, especially while hunting isn't controlled reasonably. Uncontrolled hunting can prompt populace declines and, in outrageous cases, drive species to the edge of eradication.

7. Combined and Intelligent Impacts

7.1. Synergistic Connections

Many arising dangers to bird populaces don't act in disengagement; all things being equal, they connect synergistically, enhancing their singular effects. For instance, territory misfortune can worsen the impacts of environmental change, prompting more huge disturbances in relocation examples and reproducing achievement.

7.2. Total Stressors

Bird populaces might confront different stressors at the same time, making total effects that are more extreme than the amount of individual dangers. Environmental change, contamination, territory misfortune, and different stressors can make a snare of difficulties that require far reaching and coordinated protection draws near.

8.2   Innovations in Conservation Science

Protection science, at the crossing point of environment, science, and innovation, assumes a critical part in understanding and tending to the difficulties looked by our planet's biodiversity. As of late, a rush of developments has changed the scene of preservation science, offering new instruments, techniques, and ways to deal with defend compromised species and environments. This investigation dives into key developments that are forming the fate of protection science.

1. Mechanical Headways in Observing

1.1. Remote Detecting and Satellite Innovation

The coming of remote detecting and satellite innovation has reformed the observing of biological systems for an enormous scope. Satellites outfitted with cutting edge sensors can catch high-goal symbolism, empowering researchers to survey changes in land cover, deforestation, and natural surroundings fracture. This innovation gives an exhaustive perspective on scene elements, working with more successful preservation arranging and the board.

1.2. Camera Traps and Man-made consciousness

Camera trap innovation, combined with man-made consciousness (simulated intelligence), has turned into an incredible asset for observing subtle and nighttime species. These movement enacted cameras catch pictures or recordings of natural life, and simulated intelligence calculations can then examine the information, distinguishing species and in any event, assessing populace sizes. This painless methodology improves how we might interpret untamed life conduct and dispersion.

1.3. Acoustic Observing

Propels in acoustic observing have extended our capacity to concentrate on environments by paying attention to the hints of nature. Independent recording units furnished with particular receivers can catch and examine the acoustic marks of different species. This innovation is especially important for checking avian biodiversity, including the distinguishing proof of bird species in light of their vocalizations.

2. Genomic Instruments for Preservation Hereditary qualities
2.1. Natural DNA (eDNA) Examination

Ecological DNA (eDNA) examination includes removing hereditary material from natural examples like soil, water, or air. This method gives bits of knowledge into the presence of species without direct perception. In amphibian environments, for instance, eDNA can be utilized to distinguish the presence of uncommon or subtle species, helping with the evaluation of biodiversity and illuminating preservation methodologies.

2.2. Genome Sequencing for Populace Evaluation

Headways in genome sequencing advancements have worked with top to bottom investigations of populace hereditary qualities. Understanding the hereditary variety inside populaces is urgent for powerful protection the executives. Genome sequencing permits researchers to evaluate the strength of populaces, recognize hereditarily unmistakable gatherings, and foster designated protection mediations to safeguard hereditary variety.

2.3. CRISPR Innovation for Hereditary Salvage

The progressive CRISPR-Cas9 quality altering innovation has opened up additional opportunities for hereditary salvage endeavors. In preservation, this apparatus can be applied to alleviate the effect of hereditary issues like inbreeding despondency.

Researchers might possibly alter the qualities of people or populaces to improve their strength to natural difficulties, giving a clever road to preservation hereditary qualities.

3. Local area Commitment and Resident Science
3.1. Portable Applications for Resident Science

Portable applications have changed resident science by empowering people to contribute straightforwardly to preservation endeavors. Applications, for example, iNaturalist and eBird permit clients to archive and share perceptions of natural life, contributing significant information for scientists. This inescapable commitment improves the degree and size of information assortment, transforming customary residents into preservation benefactors.

3.2. Local area Based Observing Projects

Drawing in nearby networks in protection endeavors is critical for the progress of drives. Local area based checking programs enable neighborhood occupants to partake in information assortment and the executives effectively. This approach gives important bits of knowledge into neighborhood environments as well as encourages a feeling of responsibility and stewardship among local area individuals.

4. Huge Information and Computational Environment
4.1. Information Examination for Protection Arranging

The time of large information has introduced another period for preservation science. Information examination and AI calculations can process huge datasets to distinguish designs, foresee drifts, and illuminate preservation arranging. From anticipating species conveyance to surveying the viability of safeguarded regions, these apparatuses empower proof based dynamic in preservation.

4.2. Worldwide Data sets for Biodiversity Exploration

The foundation of worldwide data sets, like the Worldwide Biodiversity Data Office (GBIF), has worked with the sharing of biodiversity information on a worldwide scale. Specialists can get to and add to these information bases, upgrading joint effort and empowering a more complete comprehension of species dispersions, ways of behaving, and communications.

5. Protection Mechanical technology and Robots
5.1. Drones for Reconnaissance and Checking

Automated airborne vehicles, or robots, have become instrumental in preservation endeavors. Drones furnished with cameras and sensors can study enormous regions rapidly and cost-really. They are utilized for undertakings like observing natural life populaces, studying distant territory, and in any event, battling poaching by giving continuous reconnaissance.

5.2. Preservation Robots for Intrusive Species Control

Intrusive species represent a huge danger to biodiversity, and imaginative arrangements are arising to address this test. Preservation robots, outfitted with computer based intelligence and advanced mechanics, can independently explore biological systems, distinguishing and killing obtrusive species. These robots offer a promising device for the designated and effective administration of obtrusive dangers.

6. Environment Demonstrating and Prescient Examination
6.1. Environment Demonstrating for Living space Reasonableness

Environment demonstrating permits researchers to extend changes in living space reasonableness for different species under various environment situations. This prescient methodology distinguishes regions that might become basic for protection later on. Protection professionals can utilize this data to focus on endeavors and lay out halls for species movement.

6.2. Prescient Examination for Preservation Arranging

Prescient examination, joined with biological demonstrating, empowers specialists to expect the effects of ecological changes on biodiversity. From anticipating the spread of sicknesses to surveying the weakness of biological systems, these apparatuses support proactive protection arranging, taking into consideration more viable alleviation and variation procedures.

7. Reclamation Environment and Manufactured Science
7.1. Biological Rebuilding Utilizing Local Species

Reclamation environment centers around restoring corrupted biological systems through the renewed introduction of local species. Progresses in how we might interpret environment elements, combined with creative procedures for seed dispersal and living space rebuilding, add to the recuperation of natural surroundings that have been affected by human exercises.

7.2. Manufactured Science for De-Annihilation Endeavors

Manufactured science offers the potential for de-annihilation endeavors, planning to resuscitate terminated species. While still in the exploratory stages, this field investigates hereditary control and particular reproducing to reproduce species that have been lost. Moral contemplations and biological ramifications are vital to conversations encompassing the use of manufactured science in preservation.

8.3 The Role of Technology in Bird Monitoring and Protection

Birds, with their different species and crucial biological jobs, are confronting various difficulties in a period set apart by fast natural changes and human exercises. Checking and safeguarding avian biodiversity have become progressively intricate undertakings that request inventive arrangements. Innovation, with its steadily developing capacities, has arisen as a strong partner in the endeavors to grasp, ration, and safeguard bird populaces. This investigation digs into the diverse job of innovation in bird observing and security, exhibiting the progressions that are forming the fate of avian protection.

1. Remote Detecting and Satellite Innovation

1.1. Outline

Remote detecting and satellite innovation have upset bird checking by giving a complete and higher perspective of scenes. Satellites outfitted with cutting edge sensors catch high-goal symbolism, empowering researchers to screen changes in land cover, vegetation, and environments for a huge scope.

1.2. Applications in Bird Checking

a. Environment Appraisal:

Satellite symbolism permits scientists to survey the degree and nature of bird environments. This is especially essential for species with explicit environment prerequisites, for example, backwoods abiding birds or wetland-subordinate species.

b. Deforestation Identification:

Checking deforestation is essential for distinguishing dangers to bird populaces. Satellites can follow changes in woodland cover, assisting traditionalists with resolving issues like territory misfortune and fracture.

c. Relocation Way Planning:

Satellite innovation helps with planning movement courses of birds. By following the development of labeled people, specialists gain bits of knowledge into movement designs, visit locales, and possible dangers en route.

1.3. Contextual analysis: Following Bird Movement with Satellites

The utilization of satellite innovation in following bird relocation is exemplified by the investigation of Cold Terns. These birds leave on perhaps of the longest relocation, going from their Icy favorable places to the Antarctic. Scaled down satellite transmitters connected to the birds give continuous information on their developments, assisting researchers with understanding the difficulties they face during this staggering excursion.

2. Camera Traps and Man-made brainpower (simulated intelligence)
2.1. Outline
Camera traps, furnished with movement sensors and high-goal cameras, offer a non-nosy technique for checking natural life. When combined with man-made brainpower (simulated intelligence), these snares can consequently recognize and arrange bird species, giving significant information to moderates.

2.2. Applications in Bird Observing
a. Subtle Species Checking:
Camera traps are especially powerful in checking slippery and nighttime bird species that are trying to concentrate on through direct perception. Man-made intelligence calculations can investigate the caught pictures, distinguishing species and assessing populace sizes.

b. Conduct Studies:
Camera traps empower scientists to direct social examinations by catching pictures or recordings of birds in their regular living spaces. This data adds to a more profound comprehension of rearing ways of behaving, settling propensities, and connections between various species.

c. Hostile to Poaching Endeavors:
As well as observing bird populaces, camera traps assume a part in enemy of poaching endeavors. They can recognize and deflect criminal operations in safeguarded regions, helping shield birds from the dangers presented by poachers.

2.3. Contextual analysis: Snow Panthers and Snowcocks
In the Himalayas, camera traps initially conveyed to screen tricky snow panthers have coincidentally caught the way of behaving of snowcocks, an inadequately concentrated on bird species. This surprising result exhibits the adaptability of camera traps in revealing important biological data past their unique objective species.

3. Acoustic Checking
3.1. Outline

Acoustic checking includes the utilization of specific hardware, like independent recording units, to catch and investigate the hints of the climate. This innovation is especially significant for observing bird vocalizations and concentrating on their ways of behaving.

3.2. Applications in Bird Checking
a. Bird Species ID:
Acoustic checking permits specialists to recognize bird species in view of their exceptional vocalizations. This is particularly valuable in regions with thick vegetation or testing landscape, where visual distinguishing proof might be unreasonable.

b. Populace Thickness Assessment:
By dissecting the recurrence and force of bird calls, researchers can assess populace densities. This data supports surveying the strength of bird populaces and recognizing areas of preservation concern.

c. Early Admonition Frameworks:
Acoustic observing can act as an early advance notice framework for the presence of explicit bird species, including those that are jeopardized or have confined conveyances. This data is critical for carrying out convenient protection mediations.

3.3. Contextual analysis: Soundscape Biology in Rainforests
In tropical rainforests, acoustic checking is utilized to concentrate on the complex soundscape made by assorted bird species. By investigating these acoustic examples, specialists gain experiences into biodiversity, biological system wellbeing, and the effects of natural surroundings aggravation.

4. Genomic Devices for Preservation Hereditary qualities
4.1. Outline
Genomic devices, including DNA examination methods, have reformed protection hereditary qualities. These devices give bits of knowledge into the hereditary variety, populace design, and strength of bird populaces.

4.2. Applications in Bird Checking
a. Natural DNA (eDNA) Investigation:
eDNA examination includes separating hereditary material from natural examples like soil, water, or air. This method can distinguish the presence of bird species without direct perception, supporting the evaluation of biodiversity.

b. Populace Wellbeing Appraisal:
Genome sequencing permits scientists to survey the soundness of bird populaces by looking at their hereditary variety. Understanding hereditary variables is urgent for successful preservation the board and staying away from issues like inbreeding sadness.

c. CRISPR Innovation for Hereditary Salvage:
The progressive CRISPR-Cas9 quality altering innovation offers the potential for hereditary salvage endeavors. Scientists can investigate ways of editting the qualities of people or populaces to improve their versatility to ecological difficulties.

4.3. Contextual investigation: California Condor Preservation
The California Condor, a basically imperiled animal categories, has profited from genomic devices in protection endeavors. Hereditary examination has informed reproducing programs, assisting with keeping up with hereditary variety and decrease the gamble of medical problems in the hostage populace.

5. Local area Commitment and Resident Science
5.1. Outline
Connecting with people in general in preservation endeavors is fundamental for building a more extensive comprehension of avian biodiversity. Innovation works with local area commitment through resident science drives and portable applications.

5.2. Applications in Bird Observing
a. Versatile Applications for Resident Science:
Versatile applications, for example, iNaturalist and eBird empower people to archive and share perceptions of birds. These applications transform birdwatchers and nature aficionados into significant supporters of logical information assortment.

b. Local area Based Observing Projects:
Local area based observing projects engage nearby occupants to partake in information assortment and the executives effectively. This approach encourages a feeling of responsibility and stewardship among local area individuals, adding to the progress of protection drives.

5.3. Contextual investigation: eBird and Worldwide Birding Patterns
eBird, a broadly utilized resident science stage, permits birdwatchers to present their perceptions on the web. The information gathered through eBird adds to logical

examination as well as gives experiences into worldwide birding patterns, distinguishing shifts in bird populaces and ways of behaving.

6. Huge Information and Computational Environment
6.1. Outline
The period of enormous information has introduced another worldview in preservation science.
Information examination and computational biology influence enormous datasets to distinguish designs, foresee drifts, and illuminate proof based independent direction.

6.2. Applications in Bird Observing
a. Information Investigation for Preservation Arranging:
AI calculations and information examination process huge datasets to distinguish designs in bird conveyances and ways of behaving. This data is urgent for creating viable preservation systems and focusing on protection activities.

b. Worldwide Information bases for Biodiversity Exploration:
Worldwide data sets like the Worldwide Biodiversity Data Office (GBIF) give a concentrated stage to sharing biodiversity information. Scientists can get to and add to these data sets, upgrading joint effort and information sharing.

6.3. Contextual investigation: Prescient Examination for Species Preservation
Prescient examination, joined with natural demonstrating, has been utilized to survey the weakness of bird species to environmental change. By examining natural factors and species appropriations, analysts can foresee likely changes in environments and plan proactive protection measures.

7. Preservation Mechanical technology and Robots
7.1. Outline
Preservation mechanical technology and robots offer creative answers for observing and safeguarding bird populaces. These advances can overview tremendous regions rapidly, gather information on distant territory, and battle dangers like poaching.

7.2. Applications in Bird Checking
a. Drones for Observation and Checking:
Outfitted with cameras and sensors, robots can overview huge regions quickly and at a lower cost than conventional strategies. They are utilized for errands, for example, observing natural life populaces, looking over settling destinations, and fighting poaching.

b. Protection Robots for Obtrusive Species Control:
Protection robots, utilizing man-made intelligence and mechanical technology, can independently explore biological systems to distinguish and take out obtrusive species. These robots offer a designated and productive method for overseeing intrusive dangers to bird living spaces.

7.3. Contextual analysis: Robot Innovation in Seabird Protection
In seabird protection, drones have been utilized to screen settling states on distant islands. This innovation gives specialists a higher perspective of settling locales, taking into consideration more precise populace evaluations and early location of possible dangers.

8. Environment Displaying and Prescient Examination
8.1. Outline
Environment displaying and prescient examination add to understanding the effects of environmental change on bird populaces. These apparatuses assist specialists with expecting shifts in territory reasonableness, relocation designs, and the dissemination of bird species.

8.2. Applications in Bird Observing
a. Environment Displaying for Territory Reasonableness:
Environment displaying empowers researchers to extend changes in territory reasonableness for bird species under various environment situations. This data distinguishes regions that might become basic for protection later on.

b. Prescient Investigation for Preservation Arranging:
Prescient investigation, joined with biological displaying, empowers analysts to expect the effects of natural changes on biodiversity. From foreseeing the spread of sicknesses to surveying the weakness of biological systems, these apparatuses support proactive preservation arranging.

8.3. Contextual analysis: Adjusting to Environmental Change in Bird Preservation
Even with environmental change, traditionalists are utilizing environment displaying to recognize regions where bird species might have to move their reaches. By understanding potential environment refugia, preservation endeavors can zero in on safeguarding these basic regions to work with species variation.

9. Rebuilding Nature and Manufactured Science
9.1. Outline

Rebuilding nature, combined with manufactured science, offers inventive ways to deal with environment restoration and species recuperation. These advancements mean to reestablish biological systems and, at times, restore terminated species.

9.2. Applications in Bird Observing
a. Natural Reclamation Utilizing Local Species:
Rebuilding nature centers around restoring corrupted environments through the renewed introduction of local species. Progresses in seed dispersal procedures and living space reclamation add to the recuperation of natural surroundings that have been affected by human exercises.

b. Manufactured Science for De-Annihilation Endeavors:
Manufactured science investigates hereditary control and particular reproducing to reproduce species that have been lost. While still in the exploratory stages, this field raises moral contemplations and environmental ramifications for potential de-annihilation endeavors.

9.3. Contextual analysis: Progressing Endeavors in Hawaiian Environment Rebuilding
In Hawaii, where many bird species are compromised by obtrusive plants and hunters, reclamation environment drives expect to reproduce local biological systems. By eliminating intrusive species and replanting local vegetation, these undertakings look to reestablish living spaces and improve conditions for local bird species.

Chapter 9
Conclusion

In the immense and perplexing embroidery of biodiversity, our planet is home to a stunning exhibit of living things, each assuming a remarkable part in the terrific ensemble of nature. As we navigate the Anthropocene, an age set apart by significant human effect on the climate, the difficulties confronting worldwide biological systems, and the different creatures inside them, have arrived at basic levels. However, in the midst of the intricacies and vulnerabilities, there arises an encouraging sign established in the aggregate endeavors of researchers, protectionists, networks, and mechanical developments. This thorough investigation digs into the complex domains of protection, advancement, and the interaction of human and biological elements, winding around together accounts of difficulties, triumphs, and the developing scene of our common obligation towards the planet.

Divulging the Natural Strings: Preservation Accounts
The accounts of protection are multifaceted and joined, recounting accounts of strength, transformation, and the fragile dance among humankind and the normal world. From the undertakings to safeguard jeopardized species and restore environments to the advancement of reasonable practices and the fashioning of protection organizations, the preservation woven artwork reflects both the victories and hardships of our common process.

Species Protection: An Orchestra of Progress and Battle
The stories of species protection reverberation the variety of life on The planet, featuring the triumphs of recuperation programs and the industrious difficulties that compromise the presence of famous and less popular living beings the same. The stories of species on the edge, like the glorious Bengal tiger and the subtle snow panther, enlighten the sensitive harmony between human exercises and the protection of biodiversity. Examples of overcoming adversity in species preservation, exemplified by the momentous recuperation of the California condor and the coordinated endeavors to safeguard ocean turtles, exhibit the positive results reachable through devoted protection drives. These accounts highlight the significance of cooperative, science-driven approaches, underlining the requirement for worldwide collaboration and local area commitment to get a future for imperiled animal types.

However, the battles endure. The dangers presented by territory misfortune, poaching, and environmental change keep on creating unfavorable shaded areas over the destiny of incalculable species. The accounts of jeopardized rhinoceroses and fundamentally imperiled pangolins represent the direness of tending to the basic drivers of termination, underscoring the requirement for comprehensive preservation systems that rise above borders and incorporate the interconnected snare of environments.

Environment Protection: Difficult exercises and Reclamation Excursions

Biological systems, the many-sided embroidered works of art woven by the connections of greenery, fauna, and the climate, structure the underpinning of life on The planet. Preservation endeavors coordinated towards safeguarding and reestablishing these perplexing frameworks unfurl stories of flexibility, variation, and the multifaceted dance between natural parts.

The Amazon rainforest, a crucial carbon sink and biodiversity area of interest, remains at the front of worldwide preservation concerns. The stories of deforestation, rapidly spreading fires, and the fragile harmony between human occupations and ecological maintainability highlight the squeezing need for approaches and practices that fit protection with the requirements of nearby networks.

Across different scenes, from the African savannahs to the coral reefs of the Pacific, protection drives endeavor to figure out some kind of harmony between human turn of events and natural safeguarding. The tales of local area based preservation, as found in the Maasai Mara and the endeavors to safeguard the Incomparable Obstruction Reef, feature the urgent job of neighborhood networks as stewards of their surroundings.

Biological system reclamation arises as an encouraging sign even with debasement. From reforestation projects in the Himalayas to the aggressive endeavors to reestablish the Aral Ocean, these accounts exhibit the groundbreaking force of biological reclamation in moderating the effects of human exercises and encouraging the recovery of once-corrupted scenes.

Advancement: Innovative Wonders and Protection Speculative chemistry

In the steadily developing scenes of science and innovation, advancement remains as a powerful power reshaping the eventual fate of protection. Mechanical wonders and spearheading approaches enlighten the pathways towards more successful, effective, and comprehensive protection techniques.

Tech Wonders in Species Checking

The domain of species checking has been changed by state of the art innovations. Satellite innovation, with its elevated perspective of scenes, uncovers the extensive vistas of living spaces and the effects of human exercises.

From following the movement of Cold Terns to surveying deforestation in the Amazon, satellite innovation gives significant bits of knowledge into the unique changes molding biological systems.

Camera traps, upgraded by computerized reasoning, offer a non-meddling focal point into the existences of slippery and nighttime species. The unintentional catch of snowcocks in the Himalayas grandstands the fortunate revelations made conceivable by these mechanical wonders, highlighting their job in revealing environmental complexities past their planned targets.

Acoustic observing, receptive to the orchestra of nature, gives a door into the vocal articulations of birds. From distinguishing species in view of their one of a kind calls to assessing populace densities, acoustic checking improves how we might interpret avian biodiversity, particularly in conditions where visual perception is testing.

Genomic Apparatuses: Disentangling the Hereditary Embroidered artwork

In the minuscule domains of hereditary qualities, creative apparatuses have uncovered the mysteries of the hereditary woven artwork that underlies the wellbeing and versatility of species. Natural DNA (eDNA) examination, a progressive strategy, permits scientists to distinguish the presence of species without direct perception, changing our capacity to survey biodiversity in different environments.

Genome sequencing, a useful asset in protection hereditary qualities, gives a nuanced comprehension of populace wellbeing and hereditary variety. The instance of the California Condor represents how genomic devices add to informed reproducing programs, moderating the dangers of inbreeding and safeguarding hereditary variety. The CRISPR-Cas9 quality altering innovation, while in its early stages, presents the chance of hereditary salvage. The possibility to alter the qualities of people or populaces offers another boondocks in preservation science, raising moral contemplations and igniting conversations about the limits of mediation.

Resident Science and Local area Commitment: Overcoming any barrier

The democratization of science through resident science and local area commitment drives changes people into dynamic members in protection attempts. Versatile applications, like iNaturalist and eBird, engage resident researchers to contribute important information, making a worldwide organization of eyewitnesses and devotees. Local area based observing projects, established in neighborhood information and stewardship, overcome any barrier between preservation objectives and the real factors looked by networks. The accounts of local area drove drives, like those in the Maasai Mara and Hawaiian biological systems, epitomize the extraordinary capability of connecting with nearby occupants in protection endeavors.

Strings of Trust: Examples Learned and Future Skylines
In the midst of the difficulties and wins, the preservation woven artwork winds around together examples learned and future skylines. As we consider the stories of species, environments, and mechanical developments, a few key topics arise, directing our way ahead.

Illustrations Took in: An Environmental Embroidered artwork of Shrewdness
1. Interconnectedness of Environments:
The stories of protection highlight the interconnectedness of biological systems and the requirement for all encompassing methodologies. The safeguarding of biodiversity requires procedures that rise above international limits and recognize the perplexing snare of collaborations molding biological frameworks.

2. Human instinct Elements:
The complicated dance between human exercises and the climate highlights the significance of thinking about the necessities and desires of neighborhood networks. Preservation systems that consolidate the points of view of native people groups and neighborhood occupants are bound to prevail in the long haul.

3. Versatile Administration:
The accounts of accomplishment and battle underscore the significance of versatile administration in preservation. Adaptability, gaining from disappointments, and changing techniques in view of advancing conditions are fundamental parts of powerful preservation rehearses.

4. Moral Contemplations in Advancement:
As mechanical advancements open new outskirts in preservation, moral contemplations become foremost. The instance of manufactured science and de-elimination endeavors brings up issues about the moral limits of intercession and the expected unseen side-effects of playing "natural chemist."

Future Skylines: Exploring the Unexplored world
1. Cooperation and Worldwide Associations:
The accounts of preservation feature the basic job of coordinated effort and worldwide associations. The difficulties confronting biodiversity rise above individual countries, requesting aggregate activity and shared liability on a worldwide scale.

2. Outfitting Innovative Advances:

The fast speed of innovative headway offers phenomenal open doors for protection. From the utilization of computerized reasoning in species observing to the likely uses of quality altering advances, what's in store holds guarantee for creative answers for squeezing protection challenges.

3. Environmental Change Versatility:

The accounts of environmental change influences on bird populaces highlight the desperation of building versatility. Protection procedures should address current dangers as well as expect and adjust to the evolving environment, guaranteeing the practicality of biological systems and the species they support.

4. Protection Training and Mindfulness:

As we explore the Anthropocene, protection schooling and mindfulness arise as vital strings in the embroidery of saving biodiversity. Cultivating a profound association with nature and imparting a feeling of obligation among people will be fundamental for building a maintainable and amicable relationship with the planet.

An Embroidery Incomplete: Future Difficulties and Potential open doors

As we stand at the junction of protection, advancement, and trust, the woven artwork of our common process stays incomplete. What's to come unfurls with the two difficulties and valuable open doors, alluring us to mesh new strings into the story of biodiversity protection.

Challenges Not too far off: Exploring Intricacy
Arising Dangers to Biodiversity

The woven artwork of preservation faces arising dangers that request dire consideration. The infringement of human exercises into normal environments, compounded by environmental change, presents uncommon difficulties. The stories of arising irresistible illnesses, intrusive species, and the complicated communications of various stressors weave a story of flexibility and weakness.

1. Natural surroundings Misfortune and Discontinuity:

As human populaces grow and scenes change, living space misfortune and fracture arise as inescapable dangers. Protection endeavors should wrestle with the outcomes of changed biological systems, looking for arrangements that offset human requirements with natural safeguarding.

2. Contamination and Its Natural Effects:

The stories of contamination, from plastic waste in seas to substance pollutants in freshwater biological systems, feature the expansive environmental effects of human-prompted contamination. Alleviating these dangers requires coordinated endeavors in squander the board, administrative measures, and public mindfulness.

3. Untamed life Exchange and Overexploitation:

The double-dealing of untamed life for the pet business, conventional medication, and different purposes stays a danger to numerous animal types. The catch and exchange of birds, particularly those with energetic plumage or special attributes, can prompt populace declines and disturb normal biological systems.

4. Overharvesting and Hunting:

Overharvesting of bird species for food, feathers, or different items can have serious ramifications for populaces, especially while hunting isn't directed reasonably. Uncontrolled hunting can prompt populace declines and, in outrageous cases, drive species to the edge of eradication.

Aggregate and Intuitive Impacts
1. Synergistic Cooperations:

Many arising dangers to bird populaces don't act in separation; all things considered, they communicate synergistically, enhancing their singular effects. For instance, living space misfortune can fuel the impacts of environmental change, prompting more huge disturbances in movement examples and rearing achievement.

2. Aggregate Stressors:

Bird populaces might confront numerous stressors all the while, making total effects that are more extreme than the amount of individual dangers. Environmental change, contamination, natural surroundings misfortune, and different stressors can make a trap of difficulties that require extensive and coordinated preservation draws near.

Protection Methodologies and Alleviation Endeavors
Territory Protection and Reclamation

Endeavors to ration and reestablish natural surroundings are critical for moderating the effects of living space misfortune and fracture. Safeguarded regions, living space passageways, and reforestation drives add to the protection and rebuilding of fundamental bird environments.

Environmental Change Alleviation and Variation

Alleviating environmental change requires worldwide endeavors to decrease ozone harming substance outflows. Also, versatile techniques, for example, establishing environment strong living spaces and helping species in acclimating to evolving conditions, are fundamental for supporting bird populaces.

Maintainable Land Use Practices

Advancing manageable land use works on, including agroforestry, natural cultivating, and capable logging, limits territory annihilation and discontinuity. Offsetting human necessities with protection objectives is crucial to accomplishing practical scenes.

Contamination Control and Backing

Endeavors to control contamination include administrative measures, squander the executives practices, and public mindfulness crusades. Promotion for strategies that focus on ecological security and diminish the utilization of destructive substances is significant for relieving contamination related dangers.

Sickness Observing and The board

Observing and overseeing illnesses in bird populaces include observation, research, and the improvement of techniques to lessen transmission. Sickness the board might incorporate immunization programs, territory rebuilding, and measures to decrease stressors that make birds more powerless to diseases.

Obtrusive Species Control

Controlling obtrusive species frequently requires a blend of destruction, control measures, and territory reclamation. Early location and fast reaction endeavors are basic for forestalling the foundation and spread of obtrusive species.

Local area Commitment and Instruction

Connecting with neighborhood networks in protection endeavors is fundamental for the progress of drives. Local area training programs, mindfulness crusades, and the inclusion of nearby partners add to a common obligation to bird preservation.

Regulation and Strategy Support

Solid ecological regulation and arrangements are fundamental for safeguarding bird populaces. Backing for the requirement and upgrade of preservation regulations, as well as the production of new defensive measures, is critical for tending to arising dangers.

Examination and Checking

Proceeded with research on bird populaces, their ways of behaving, and the effects of arising dangers is fundamental for informed preservation procedures. Observing projects that track populace patterns, dissemination, and wellbeing give fundamental information to preservation direction.

9.1   Recap of the Importance of Birds in Sustaining Biodiversity

As we explore the mind boggling scenes of biodiversity, the job of birds arises as a key part in keeping up with the sensitive equilibrium of biological systems. From the transcending shelters of tropical rainforests to the immense breadths of bone-dry deserts, avian species add to the strength, usefulness, and magnificence of the regular world. This recap dives into the diverse significance of birds in supporting biodiversity, featuring their natural, social, and financial importance.

1. Biological system Administrations: Past Tune and Plumage
1.1. Fertilization Elements

Birds, frequently decorated with dynamic plumage and sweet tunes, assume a vital part in the fertilization of blooming plants. As they scrounge for nectar, they incidentally move dust starting with one blossom then onto the next, working with the multiplication of innumerable plant species. This biological help guarantees the progression of plant populaces as well as adds to the creation of foods grown from the ground that support a different exhibit of untamed life.

Model: Hummingbirds and Orchids

Hummingbirds, with their specific long bills and floating capacities, structure unpredictable associations with orchids. The special design of orchid blossoms lines up with the life systems of hummingbirds, encouraging a commonly valuable organization. As hummingbirds feed on nectar, they coincidentally move dust, advancing the hereditary variety and strength of orchid populaces.

1.2. Seed Dispersal Instruments

Birds, through their taking care of ways of behaving, assume a significant part in seed dispersal. Ingesting seeds from different plants, birds transport them to various areas, adding to the colonization of new environments and the recovery of biological systems. This cycle is especially fundamental in regions where the normal dispersal systems of plants are restricted.

Model: Frugivorous Birds and Tropical Woodlands

In tropical rainforests, frugivorous birds, like toucans and hornbills, consume leafy foods seeds across the backwoods covering.

This powerful interaction upholds the variety of plant species and adds to the general wellbeing and design of these biodiverse biological systems.

2. Adjusting Biological Elements
2.1. Bother Control and Bug Guideline
Birds are regular controllers of bug populaces, adding to the control of vermin that can in any case wreck crops and upset environments. Insectivorous birds, like swallows, songbirds, and flycatchers, assume a basic part in keeping a harmony among hunter and prey, forestalling flare-ups of unsafe bugs.

Model: Purple Martins and Agrarian Advantages
Purple Martins are prestigious for their flying trapeze artistry and bug getting ability. Ranchers have perceived the advantages of drawing in Purple Martins to their fields, as these birds assist with controlling bug bothers, diminishing the requirement for substance pesticides and advancing feasible rural practices.

2.2. Biodiversity Pointers
The presence and overflow of bird species act as dependable signs of environment wellbeing and biodiversity. Changes in bird populaces can flag more extensive natural movements, giving early alerts of ecological aggravations, territory debasement, or the presentation of obtrusive species.

Model: Shorebirds and Wetland Environments
Shorebirds, including sandpipers and plovers, are delicate to changes in wetland environments. Their populaces mirror the wellbeing of seaside regions, with decreases in bird numbers frequently showing dangers like environment misfortune, contamination, or disturbances in food accessibility. Observing these pointers permits researchers and moderates to carry out ideal mediations to shield wetland biodiversity.

3. Social Importance: Associating People group to Nature
3.1. Imagery and Folklore
Birds have held emblematic importance in assorted societies and legends all through mankind's set of experiences. Their presence in fables, writing, and workmanship mirrors a profound and persevering through association among people and the avian world. From the superb falcon representing opportunity to the savvy owl addressing information, birds enhance social stories and customs.

Model: Crane Imagery in East Asian Societies
In East Asian societies, cranes are adored images of life span, devotion, and satisfaction.

The Japanese red-delegated crane, known as the "tancho," holds specific social significance and is viewed as an image of favorable luck. The preservation of crane populaces is interlaced with social works on, cultivating a common obligation to their prosperity.

3.2. Birdwatching and Ecotourism

The perception of birds, known as birdwatching, has developed into a worldwide side interest and a foundation of ecotourism. Devotees and travelers the same search out avian areas of interest, adding to neighborhood economies and encouraging a feeling of appreciation for normal scenes. This ecotourism-driven interest in birds makes monetary motivations for protection endeavors and supports the conservation of crucial natural surroundings.

Model: Transient Bird Celebrations

Transient bird celebrations, held in different regions of the planet, commend the sensational excursions of birds across landmasses. These celebrations not just give open doors to birdwatchers to observe momentous avian exhibitions yet additionally advance mindfulness about the significance of saving visit locales and environments basic for transitory species.

4. Financial Commitments: Padded Resources

4.1. Rural Advantages

Birds contribute straightforwardly to rural efficiency through bother control administrations. By consuming bugs that present dangers to crops, birds diminish the requirement for synthetic pesticides, prompting cost reserve funds for ranchers and advancing feasible cultivating rehearses. This natural help improves crop yields and supports food security.

Model: Animal dwellingplace Swallows and Agrarian Vermin Control

Animal dwellingplace swallows, known for their unmistakable forked tails, are unquenchable bug purchasers. They assume an essential part in controlling flying bugs, including farming nuisances. The presence of outbuilding swallows in ranch scenes adds to a characteristic bug the executives framework, helping the two ranchers and environments.

4.2. The travel industry and Sporting Open doors

Birdwatching the travel industry has turned into a huge financial driver in numerous districts. The presence of assorted bird species draws in sightseers, birdwatchers, and nature fans, making income streams for nearby networks.

Safeguarded regions and natural life saves that help rich birdlife frequently become magnets for ecotourism, encouraging financial development while advancing preservation.

Model: Costa Rica's Birdwatching The travel industry

Costa Rica, prestigious for its excellent biodiversity, has exploited birdwatching the travel industry as a foundation of its ecotourism industry. The country's different environments have a momentous assortment of bird species, drawing birdwatchers from around the world. This inundation of ecotourists adds to the nearby economy and highlights the monetary benefit of protecting regular territories.

5. Protection Difficulties and Goals

5.1. Environment Misfortune and Fracture

The overall test confronting bird populaces is natural surroundings misfortune and fracture. As human exercises change scenes for agribusiness, urbanization, and foundation improvement, the normal environments fundamental for birds are compromised. Protection endeavors should focus on the conservation and rebuilding of these living spaces to guarantee the endurance of different avian species.

Basic: Environment Preservation and Reclamation Drives

Shielding bird environments requires a multi-layered approach, including the production of safeguarded regions, living space reclamation projects, and feasible land-use rehearses. Cooperation between states, preservation associations, and neighborhood networks is basic to address the underlying drivers of environment misfortune and carry out successful protection procedures.

5.2. Environmental Change Effects

Environmental change represents a critical danger to bird populaces, influencing movement designs, reproducing seasons, and the accessibility of reasonable living spaces. Climbing temperatures, adjusted precipitation examples, and outrageous climate occasions challenge the flexibility of bird species. Protection drives should incorporate environmental change flexibility techniques to relieve the effects on avian biodiversity.

Basic: Environment Versatile Protection Practices

Preservation systems ought to integrate environment strong methodologies, including the distinguishing proof and assurance of environment refugia, the making of passageways for species development, and the advancement of natural surroundings variety.

By tending to the interconnected difficulties of living space misfortune and environmental change, protection endeavors can improve the capacity of bird populaces to endure ecological tensions.

5.3. Human-Natural life Clashes and Protection Morals

As human populaces extend and connect with regular living spaces, clashes among birds and human exercises might emerge. These struggles incorporate rivalry for assets, predation on yields, and unsettling influences to settling locales. Protection drives should explore these contentions morally, taking into account the necessities of both human networks and bird species.

Basic: People group Commitment and Moral Preservation Practices

Connecting with neighborhood networks in preservation dynamic cycles is vital for cultivate understanding and participation. By coordinating customary information and practices into preservation procedures, drives can address human-natural life clashes in manners that help both biodiversity and local area prosperity. Moral contemplations ought to direct mediations, guaranteeing that protection endeavors are conscious of the different requirements and points of view, everything being equal.

6. Looking Forward: A Common Obligation regarding Avian Biodiversity

In the great embroidery of biodiversity, birds arise as energetic strings, winding around together biological systems, societies, and economies. As we ponder the significance of birds in supporting biodiversity, a common obligation arises — one that rises above lines, disciplines, and individual interests. The difficulties are considerable, however the valuable open doors for positive change proliferate.

6.1. Global Coordinated effort and Strategy Promotion

The protection of avian biodiversity requests global coordinated effort and strategy promotion. Transient bird species, specifically, navigate mainlands, requiring composed endeavors to address dangers all through their whole reach. Peaceful accords, like the Ramsar Show on Wetlands and the Show on Transitory Species, give systems to cooperative activity and strategy advancement.

6.2. Training and Public Mindfulness

Training and public mindfulness are mainstays of successful bird preservation. Outreach programs, school drives, and media missions can cultivate a more profound comprehension of the biological jobs of birds and the significance of saving their territories. By ingraining a feeling of marvel and obligation towards birds, these endeavors add to a social shift towards additional feasible practices.

6.3. Logical Exploration and Mechanical Developments
Logical exploration and mechanical advancements are vital apparatuses in the preservation tool compartment. Propels in following advances, satellite checking, and genomic research upgrade how we might interpret bird conduct, biology, and populace elements. The joining of resident science further democratizes research endeavors, enrolling the general population in information assortment and checking drives.

6.4. Feasible Advancement Practices
Feasible improvement rehearses are principal in accomplishing an agreeable conjunction among people and birds. Adjusting the necessities of networks with protection objectives requires the advancement of manageable land use, mindful the travel industry, and eco-accommodating rural practices. By adjusting financial advancement to environmental stewardship, we can make scenes that benefit the two individuals and birds.

6.5. Preservation Morals and Social Regard
Protection morals, established in social regard and moral contemplations, guide the moral treatment of birds and their territories. Perceiving the social meaning of birds and regarding native information frameworks are fundamental components of moral protection. By consolidating assorted viewpoints and values, preservation drives can be more comprehensive, impartial, and powerful.

9.2   Call to Action for Conservation and Sustainable Practices
Even with heightening dangers to avian biodiversity, a resonating source of inspiration reverberations through the passageways of preservation. Earnest and aggregate endeavors are basic to protect the significant commitments of birds to our planet's environmental, social, and monetary embroidery. People, people group, and countries should join in a promise to preservation and feasible practices.
The source of inspiration starts with encouraging a profound comprehension of the complicated jobs birds play in keeping up with environment concordance. Schooling and public mindfulness drives are crucial, imparting a feeling of obligation and miracle toward avian biodiversity. Worldwide cooperation and strategy promotion are fundamental for address worldwide difficulties, especially for transient species that cross lines.

Economical improvement rehearses, directed by moral contemplations and social regard, structure the foundation of capable stewardship. This includes advancing eco-accommodating agribusiness, mindful the travel industry, and maintainable land-use rehearses. Mechanical advancements and logical examination engage these undertakings, giving essential experiences to informed direction.

As watchmen of our common planet, we are called to orchestrate our activities with the ensemble of wings, guaranteeing an inheritance where birds flourish, environments prosper, and the interconnected strings of biodiversity weave a strong embroidery for a long time into the future. The source of inspiration isn't simply an obligation; it is a common obligation to saving the magnificence and equilibrium of our regular world.